4/95

D0791373

# TIMBER
# REDUCED
# ENERGY
# EFFICIENT
# HOMES

**T** TIMBER
**R** REDUCED
**E** ENERGY
**E** EFFICIENT
HOMES

Ed Paschich and Paula Hendricks

Photographs by Paula Hendricks

Illustrations by Ed Paschich

SUNSTONE PRESS

SANTA FE
NEW MEXICO

## ACKNOWLEDGEMENT

*I would like to thank
Jack, my father,
for having faith in me
and letting me build our
first solar adobe house.*

Ed Paschich

## IMPORTANT NOTE TO READER

We've provided a great deal of information about building design, techniques, practices and products in this book. In most cases, we've relied on our own experiences as well as research and recommendations by others whose knowledge and judgement we respect. However, we can't and don't guarantee the results. This book offers you a start. The responsibility for using it ultimately rests with you.

■

© 1994 by Ed Paschich
Photographs © 1994 by Paula Hendricks

All Rights Reserved

No part of this book may be reproduced in any form or by any electronic or mechanical means including information storage and retrieval systems, without permission in writing from the publisher, except by a reviewer who may quote brief passages in a review.

First edition
Printed in the United States of America

10   9   8   7   6   5   4   3   2   1

Library of Congress Cataloging in Publication Data

Paschich, Ed, 1950-
    Timber reduced energy efficient homes / Ed Paschich and Paula Hendricks ; photographs by Paula Hendricks, illustrations by Ed Paschich. -- 1st ed.
        p.   cm/
    Tree homes appears as a title per typography on t.p.
    Includes bibliographical references and index.
    ISBN: 0-86534-208-3 : $17.95
    1. Dwellings--Energy Conservation. 2. Timber. 3. Conservation of natural resources. I. Hendricks, Paula. II. Title. III. Title: Tree homes.
    TJ163.5.D86P38    1994
    696--dc20                                   93-35704
                                                    CIP

Published by Sunstone Press
        Post Office Box 2321
        Santa Fe, New Mexico 87504-2321 / USA

696
PAS
1993

# Table of Contents

# List of Plates

# INTRODUCTION

For years many people have been trying to raise awareness about the limits of our natural world and how we are using up our resources faster than they can be replaced. We are cutting down trees at a phenomenal rate, pulling minerals out of the earth, using up petroleum reserves and at the same time filling the air, the ground and the water we drink with pollutants. We are dumping our garbage into land fills faster than we can manage them. All in all, not something to be proud of. We know all this, and more, from reading the newspapers any day of the week. The situation is not good, from a variety of standpoints:

- We are an ecosystem with the earth and ultimately what is good, or bad, for the earth is good, or bad, for us.

- Our continued neglect of cause and effect, of long-term and long-range implications of manufacturing, mining, reduction of forest lands, and use of chemicals is damaging to our own health and our children's.

- It is simply wrong to continue to damage our environment when we know better and can change our behavior to be less destructive.

However, the environmentally responsible choices in life are often easier and most times less expensive, and recycled materials often cost less, and sometimes are even free. Many of us know things have to change. And they are changing... slowly. There is a growing awareness and sensitivity to environmental issues, mostly from concerned citizens, people like you and me. It's up to us to do what we can. We must recycle our papers, our aluminum cans, our plastics, and not ask for a bag every time we buy something.

And a very big thing we can do is make changes smart for us and smart for the environment when we fix up, repair, renovate, or build new homes. There are literally hundreds of ways to make our homes less harmful to the environment—and we can do this at little or no extra cost, with readily available construction materials, in an aesthetically pleasing way.

Here in New Mexico, we are fortunate to have easy access to ancient dwellings that still stand, cliff dwellings such as those at Mesa Verde in southern Colorado, and man-made masonry cities such as those at Chaco Canyon in northern New Mexico. The old ways can lead us to new ways—an alliance between working with nature *and* man-made technology.

Figure 1:1 [left]
Anasazi cliff dwellings at Mesa Verde, Colorado.

A concept for building homes that reduces impact on the environment has been developed by Passage Construction Company, Inc. of Corrales, New Mexico based on their pursuit of environmentally responsible building design and techniques. They have refined their concept while building solar heated homes over the past seventeen years, and identified it as the "T.R.E.E. Home," which stands for Timber Reduced Energy Efficient Home. These homes are designed and built to use timber more efficiently, eliminate the destruction of large old trees, and to utilize other building materials that consume less energy overall, and are less harmful to the environment.

This book is about what we can do, as average everyday people who want to live in familiar, traditional-looking homes. Who want quality that will last, low utility and low maintenance bills. To have a house that will resell easily. To be sensitive to the earth's health and depletion of her natural resources. To take a reasonable, rational, pragmatic approach to building.

This book is also about choices, what questions to ask, and to encourage the use of the most readily renewable resources for building. The questions become complicated—how to balance renewable resources against cost, against future maintenance, against pollution in manufacturing and installing, as well as using the best material for the job—so the answers are not always the obvious ones and it becomes very personal. Our recommendations may advocate the use of less desirable materials from time to time, but they are based on an assessment and balance of risks as well as cost effectiveness. For example, we advocate the use of rigid foam insulation and noxious sealers because they remain the best products readily available at reasonable cost.

But, balance is sought. And this is an on-going process. A few years from now there will be more choices. As we (all of us who build homes) continue to ask our suppliers for recycled carpet and tile, as we continue to use more cellulose insulation, manufacturers will respond with even better choices than we have available to us today. Louisiana-Pacific is building two big cellulose plants, investing millions, in response to these demands and their belief this will be a profitable investment for them. Also, building codes and zoning regulations govern choices. Every community has its own set of rules and regulations, and the experiences, shared in the book, reflect those primarily of New Mexico. While most of the information here will be relevant in virtually every part of the country, be sure to become familiar with your own community's codes and regulations. You may even have a few options available to you that are better than what we have available.

Choices were made, for this book, and in the everyday building of T.R.E.E. Homes, that use materials readily available in the construction industry, that can be worked with easily. Methods were used that have been proven to work over time.

Yet, the experimental has its place, too. Fixtures and systems are used that have easily replaceable parts (the kind supply houses keep in stock). Where it makes sense, recycled materials are chosen, and recycling during the building process is on-going. Most of all, the homes built are of enduring quality, are easy to maintain, and retain their value, character, and charm through the years.

Choices can be as simple as planting a deciduous tree on the south side of the house to help cool the house during the hot summer months to building an entire house system that includes precise site orientation, recycling of rain water, composting, and using gray water for irrigation.

This book is not THE ANSWER. There is no one, right, answer. But, it is a start, and we hope you can benefit from our experiences. Browse through the book, or read it cover to cover. We all do what we can...and these techniques are something we've learned over the years. And you can use them, too.

Ed Paschich and Paula Hendricks
Corrales, New Mexico, 1993

CHAPTER 1

AN OVERVIEW

For most of us our homes are a significant investment—both in terms of money as well as time. We invest in our homes financially and emotionally. And most of us live in a particular house for a significant length of time. We buy or build a home, we fix it up, replace the windows, add a room, do a major renovation. And more and more of us are building homes, new ones, customized to our individual needs and lifestyles. Today, our homes can be more than a good investment, a good neighborhood, a good school. They can reflect us, who we are, what we care about—and we can improve our homes and do less damage to our natural world than we've done in the past.

The world seems to be a more complicated place than it used to be—even when it comes to the environment. In the 1970s it seemed solar power was the answer. If we'd all just use solar energy we would be on the road to recovery. But, we aren't. It's not that simple. Now we need to reduce air pollution, reduce our use of materials that deplete the ozone layer and contribute to the greenhouse effect. Adding to the confusion is recent speculation that the depletion of the ozone layer may be beneficially tied to reducing the adverse effects of global warming. And global warming may be a beneficial natural response to a not-so-future ice age. So, the choices of which products to buy, which insulation, how much concrete to use, are made more complicated—do we buy something that does not reduce ozone levels *and* does not contribute to global warming and

*As we continue to eliminate species and habitats we will surely affect our own lives in basic and unknown ways.*

does not contaminate the earth, the air, the ground water—are there ways to know how to make these choices?

Look at our recommendations in this book. Do they make sense for you, your lifestyle, for the type of house you have or want to have? Does your community have codes and regulations that allow use of innovative techniques or are the codes more restrictive? Don't follow this book blindly. Use it as a starting point. Then, ask questions. Talk to your local contractors. There are no "pure" answers. Some of our recommendations do, indeed, pollute the atmosphere a small amount; we do make recommendations that are slightly damaging to our environment, but they are less damaging than many standard practices, and they are the best options available to us at the current time.

We have evaluated all our building materials based on their functional qualities as well as their impact on the environment. When determining our recommendations for a T.R.E.E. Home we have taken into account the following primary areas of concern:

- Reduction of Forest Lands
- Global Warming
- Ozone Depletion
- Chemicals in Processing
- Pollution—Acid Rain, Garbage, et al.
- Recycling
- Use of Hazardous Materials
- Use of Non-Renewable Resources/Energy
- Zoning, Codes & Regulations

## REDUCTION OF FOREST LANDS

We are using up forest timber faster than we are replacing it. We are still cutting down trees and not allowing or providing for new growth to start or continue. It has been estimated that only 15% of the old forests in this country remain standing today. Trees that have lived for a thousand years are being cut and most "old growth" could be gone within a generation. This is unsatisfactory because forests contribute significantly to the manufacture and balance of oxygen in the environment. Trees absorb carbon dioxide, which helps balance the greenhouse effect (what keeps the earth warm and sustainable of human life), keeping the atmosphere temperate. These forests provide humidity and help purify groundwater. They provide habitats for many species of animals, birds, insects and other plants. By mis-managing the forests we destroy more than we know. We cause erosion, and destruction of untold numbers of animal and plant species. The killing of the last of anything is a moral issue—but we all exist in a vast, complex biosphere. As we continue to eliminate species and habitats we will surely affect our own lives in basic and unknown ways. Wilderness areas are also good for the soul—providing beauty and recreation for many of us.

The controversy over the rainforests in various parts of the world is particularly striking and frightening. The rainforests have been called nature's laboratory. While they cover only 2% of the Earth's surface (near the equator in Africa, South America, Central America, and Asia), more than 50% of all the wild plants, animals and insects live in them, and 25% of all pharmaceuticals come from plants in tropical rainforests. Only 1% of these plants have ever been studied. The National Cancer Institute has identified plants useful in the treatment of cancer, and approximately 70% of them are found only in rainforests. It is estimated that 40% of the earth's oxygen is produced in the rainforests of Amazonia. Deforestation is proceeding at an alarming rate—40% of the tropical rainforests in Latin America and Asia are already gone, and 80% of the cutting in Amazonia alone has taken place since 1980.

In the southwestern part of the United States, some of our traditional building styles have been quite efficient—building small houses with small rooms required shorter spans and used

Figure 1:2 [above]
*Casa Vieja* (Old House) in Corrales, New Mexico. This building was a church originally built between 1706 and 1712.

*Because forests are renewable and can be managed to produce and reproduce high quality timber in relatively short time frames, we need to actively pursue establishment and use of timber from tree farms and sustainable managed forests, and we must continue to lobby against clear-cutting.*

locally available materials, in this case smaller logs. In New Mexico locally available materials also means earth—adobe. And many of these structures are hundreds of years old. [See Figure 1:2.]

As people began building larger rooms, and larger houses, bigger logs were used as support beams (vigas) and support posts. Many of these logs have diameters of 18" or more. In the 1950s, builders' demands for square beams increased as they were easier to build with and to sheetrock over. To get a 6" x 10" square beam, a tree with a diameter of 18" at breast height has to be cut, and that demands cutting old trees. A hundred-year-old, 60' tall ponderosa pine with a breast height diameter of 14" is too small for standard 2" x 12" beams used in the building of a standard frame house. It is estimated that 80% of the beams for ceilings, even the exposed ones, in the American Southwest are square.

This situation was made very clear to us early on—we had been using 8" x 12"s and their delivery, once, was delayed. We called the sawmill and were told they had to search out some old trees so they could get logs big enough for our 8" x 12"s. We felt awful. We have since developed designs and techniques that use logs of no more than 9" that can be grown on tree farms in seven years.

While overall the picture is bleak, there are bright spots—some forests are being managed responsibly and some forests are not over-harvested (particularly in Canada). In fact, there are forests that are growing faster than they are being harvested. This confirms our belief that forests and lumber can continue to provide us with high quality products at a reasonable cost in terms of both money and the environment. Because forests are renewable and can be managed to produce and reproduce high quality timber in relatively short time frames, we need to actively pursue establishment and use of timber from tree farms and sustainable managed forests, and we must continue to lobby against clear-cutting.

We can avoid use of exotic wood, unless certified that the wood is from sustainable managed forests, and we can choose woods (when wood is the best product) that are produced in tree farms and are of species that are not overharvested. And we buy all our wood products from the Forest Trust, a division of the Tides Foundation. The Forest Trust Wood Products

Brokerage is a non-profit organization that provides contractors in northern New Mexico with a complete line of high quality, Southwest style, wood building materials. They promote environmentally and economically sound forest practices on New Mexico's private and public lands. The lumber is all harvested locally and includes spruce, Douglas fir, white fir and pine.

Pine is widely used because there is so much available and it is a strong, straight wood. However, it is slow-growing. Compared with pine, aspen and spruce are plentiful, faster-growing woods and are increasingly being used. Aspen is used in manufactured products like laminated strand lumber (an upgrade of OSB, oriented strand board). Spruce has a good strength-to-weight ratio, but it is more susceptible to moisture, warping, checking, cracking, and cupping. It deforms from moisture more easily than pine. Spruce is not overharvested, yet.

Other woods such as redwood and cedar are over-harvested, but they also offer special properties—we might use these woods only where their weathering properties are essential and use other woods when those properties are not necessary.

## GLOBAL WARMING

As mentioned, the greenhouse effect is what keeps the earth warm and sustainable of human life. If it goes out of balance we could have another ice age or an atmosphere too hot for comfortable living. About half of the global warming problem is due to the increase in carbon dioxide in the atmosphere, and this is attributed primarily to the reduction of forests and the burning of fossil fuels. Following are other significant contributors to global warming:

- **Chlorofluorocarbons (CFCs)** and **hydrochlorofluorocarbons (HCFCs)** contribute 15-20% to global warming. They are present in rigid foam insulation (ISO and polystyrene) and refrigeration (freon is almost pure CFCs).

- **Methane** contributes approximately 18% to global warming and is produced by cattle, rice fields, and landfills.

- **Nitrous oxide** contributes about 10% to global warming and is produced by microbes breaking down chemical fertilizers and burning wood and fossil fuels.

What is desired is balance—and to do no damage.

## OZONE DEPLETION

The ozone layer shields the earth from the sun's harmful ultra-violet rays. Without the ozone layer, we would be much more susceptible to getting skin cancers, cataracts, and to having our immune systems suppressed. Ultra-violet radiation also reduces crop yields and fish populations. This protective shield is damaged most by CFCs, HCFCs, halons, and other man-made chemicals that break down in the upper atmosphere. The breakdown of CFCs releases chlorine, and each molecule of chlorine destroys more than 100,000 molecules of ozone. CFCs and HCFCs are particularly dangerous because they are so stable—they do not decompose easily or fast, and they last for one hundred fifty years or more. So we face not only the effects of our current and future behavior, but also the problem of handling chemicals already in the upper atmosphere that are very, very slowly decomposing. It is estimated that 3-5% of the ozone layer has already been destroyed by CFCs. Again, balance is sought to minimize any damage we cause by our choices.

## CHEMICALS IN PROCESSING

Most everything we use has been processed. Wood is processed—by cutting, treating, sealing—depending on its purpose. Plywood is, obviously, processed as are support posts and woods like osmose. Osmose is wood treated with liquid strychnine, a preservative used primarily to prevent rot. Burning this wood releases the strychnine and creates yet another danger. Concrete, plastic, glass, metal products, paint, stucco, roofing materials—all are processed to one degree or another. A critical part of the process involves the use of chemicals. The use of energy is discussed later.

These chemicals are of concern in terms of potential harm
to the workers at plants, as waste by-products introduced into
the air, water or ground (including solid waste dumped in
landfills), as well as potential hazards in handling the processed product and any future seepage or deterioration during
the life use of the product. Industrialized nations produce more
than 70,000 chemicals, and many of them end up as hazardous
waste and/or pollutants in our air and groundwater.

Since the late 1800s, at least, we have believed we have
unlimited resources (here in America and world-wide) and
that—no matter what we do—we really can't damage the environment. After all, it's been here for millions of years. We have
believed in man over nature, in technology, in machines and
man-made chemicals. But we are waking up, slowly. It's time
we took a more balanced approach. Sometimes the least-pro-
cessed materials are the best, and sometimes compromise is
necessary—and the use of processed materials is the best choice.
We make specific recommendations with the understanding
that we have chosen the best possible products for the job that
also do the least damage to our environment.

Albuquerque Academy
Library
6400 Wyoming Blvd. N.E.
Albuquerque, N.M.  87109

## POLLUTION

Pollution. It's almost impossible to know where to begin
with this subject or how to provide a simple overview of it.
Dirty air, toxic earth, tainted water...it's everywhere. And some
days it feels like it's caused by everything we do—even breath-
ing out. All of this is true—we produce pollutants just by living.
But over the last fifty years or more we—particularly those of us
in the industrialized world—have become dangerously extravagant in our production of pollutants. The very basis of our
political, military, and industrial strength is also the basis of our
seriously polluted environment. Smog, acid rain, undrinkable
groundwater, contaminated earth unfit for building upon let
alone living near. The list goes on and on. Sometimes the culprit
is large and newsworthy—nuclear plants, nuclear waste, the
Love Canal, Rocky Flats and the controversial WIPP site in New
Mexico. Whole neighborhoods near the Love Canal in upstate
New York became uninhabitable due to the high levels of toxic
waste found in the land and water. Defense contractors at the

Rocky Flats nuclear facility in Colorado are accused of illegally dumping radioactive waste—in large amounts—over many years. WIPP is the Waste Isolation Pilot Plant (an underground storage facility for "low level" radioactive waste) the US Government is planning to open in Carlsbad, New Mexico. The controversy concerns the transportation of radioactive waste and waste storage in the salt caverns of southern New Mexico. Many people do not believe adequate safety measures and long-term effects have been taken into account. They do not wish New Mexico to become another Love Canal. But, sometimes the culprits are small and manageable—choices over which paint to use and how to dispose of the unused portions.

We make recommendations in this book about products that pollute the least and still do the best job. To reach these recommendations we took into account pollutants created during the "mining," or original processing, of the raw materials, as well as pollutants resulting from the manufacturing, shipping, installing, and life-use of the final products. We also make suggestions about maintenance that will help each of us reduce pollutants and garbage in our own environments.

Acid rain is another form of pollution and destruction—it damages trees, wildlife (animal and vegetable) and pollutes the air, the water, the earth. In many ways acid rain is a new threat—like global warming and ozone depletion. Acid rain is caused primarily by sulfur dioxide and nitrogen oxide, gasses released into the atmosphere by coal-burning power plants (which contribute approximately 65% of the sulfur dioxide emissions in the US) and by automobiles.

What we can do is use less electricity and choose products that use less electricity at all stages of their lives and are made close to home (less shipping means less motor vehicle emissions).

## GARBAGE

Humans have always made garbage. To archaeologists, the midden heaps (garbage dumps) are gold mines. But in today's world, garbage is getting out of hand. We have been a wasteful nation. We have believed we had unlimited resources. There has always been this mythical sense that we have more than enough for all of us. Operating on this myth has made us greedy. We want more, more than we have, and more than we need. We throw things away, and we create extravagant amounts of waste. Other industrialized nations produce half as much trash per person as we do in the United States. We realize we cannot continue creating all this waste, nor can we continue using up our limited resources without thought. There are limits.

We have always looked for the easiest and cheapest way out. If we apply this approach to garbage, it would mean produce less and recycle more—tenets we, as builders, fully believe in and apply to our building practices.

## RECYCLING

Nature is virtually a continual recycling process and all the plants and animals on earth are involved in the process, from lions and tigers to termites and fungi. Humans have always been part of this natural process. But, we have become lazy and have developed processes that make recycling increasingly difficult. Products made more durable by man-made technologies have also been made practically impervious to destruction.

Humans have always recycled rare and valuable resources; bones from animals were recycled as spoons and weapons; gold has been always been recycled, it's rarely thrown away. In addition to recycling paper and plastic from our garbage cans, and sorting glass and aluminum cans for our community recycling centers, we are beginning to see and buy other recycled products—packaging from recycled cardboard, recycled stationery and insulation. This process can go much, much further. We can recycle our own construction materials, and we can buy more and more recycled products for use as structural materials in our building projects—recycled tile and carpet, recycled bricks, recycled plastics. And we can recycle those things we cannot use easily ourselves: brick, lumber, dirt, cement block, even sheetrock. These things can be salvaged for others' use and/or used for clean fill (waste that will not release toxic gasses, liquids, fumes in the process of disintegrating, or that is toxic to begin with). Oil, tires, and batteries are not "clean".

Recycling should simply become a way of thinking. The

*We have always looked for the easiest and cheapest way out. If we apply this approach to garbage, it would mean produce less and recycle more.*

*We can encourage our suppliers, and ultimately the manufacturers, to provide us with even more alternatives in terms of innovative recycled products.*

very first question should be: Can we get what we want from recycled products? Can it be recycled when we're done with it? We can encourage our suppliers, and ultimately the manufacturers, to provide us with even more alternatives in terms of innovative recycled products.

## USE OF HAZARDOUS MATERIALS

We have stopped using lead-based paints. We are removing asbestos insulating tiles from ceilings and are no longer using asbestos where we might come in contact with it. As a society we are waging war on cigarette smoke and smoking, and some would say we are winning that war. Hazardous materials are all around us. Some are natural and some are man-made. Hazardous plants are common: digitalis, columbine, oleander, to name just a few. For years many of us drank water that was chlorinated and treated with fluoride. Now, we sift water through filters, often to remove the chlorine and fluoride. For many years we have been making, and dumping, without thought, incredible numbers and amounts of hazardous materials into landfills and our own backyards.

## USE OF NON-RENEWABLE RESOURCES

Oil, natural gas, coal, and minerals become plastics, energy, nails, and rebar. Practically everything we do use involves one or more of these resources, and this is particularly true when building a home. Minerals are the smallest issue, even though our use of these products diminishes a finite resource—metals are recycled regularly, and there is little loss in the recycling process. The more precious the metal, the easier it is to recycle.

Oil, coal, and gas are not recycled easily as they change composition during use, and they pollute the environment as well. As these resources are diminished, they will also become more expensive. So, alternatives are desirable, both short term and longer term. We look for ways to reduce our dependence on "imported energy" by using "free" resources, such as the sun, as much as possible. Energy use is a primary criteria in our analyses of building materials. We have examined, in some detail, energy use at various stages of a products' life—from mining/gathering, through processing, shipping, and ultimate use over time. We have searched out products and building methods that use less energy at every stage.

## ZONING

Codes and regulations are enacted to ensure safe housing. The safety of the home's inhabitants is assured when electrical outlets are grounded. Structural codes are designed to prevent accidents and fires, but many codes are in place because of lobbying by building industry manufacturers. Some speculate, for example, that houses could be cheaper and just as stable by using fewer support studs, but codes often specify wasteful practices.

Politics influence codes, too...as do hurricanes in Florida, and earthquakes in California. In New Mexico we can build houses made of dirt, or tires. We can also build frame houses and houses of stone. A few years ago you could not build a traditional adobe (mud bricks dried in the sun, or the mud from which the bricks are made) house in California. You could fill standard frame cavities with dirt, but you could not use adobe bricks.

When you decide to build or renovate a home, check your local, county and state agencies. And contact a contractor who is knowledgeable. ■

# 2 CHAPTER

## QUALITY and STYLE OF LIFE

Figure 2:1 [below right]
Interior adobe walls in round Great Room.

Figure 2:2 [below left]
Interior frame wall with linear detail.

Beyond the basics, the necessities of life, is an issue some consider equally important: the quality of life. While it is important to make sure the basic systems function well and reliably, and while we are doing things that are good for the environment and our budgets, to many of us the quality of our living spaces is a significant part of our satisfaction with life. These are individual preferences. To one, absolute quiet during any time of the day or night in at least one room is of primary importance. To another, an open, flowing, light-filled house is a must.

Many people who live in adobe houses fall in love with them, with their perception of mass, warmth and movement. Some speculate that adobe houses trigger genetic memories of cave dwellings, with their sense of safety and comfort. The mass of the adobe walls seems to breathe, to move with the earth itself. There is a comfort that comes from simply sitting close to an adobe wall. Perhaps, it is a sense of protection, of mothering. [See Figure 2.1.]

Others prefer log houses or the more traditional sense of a frame house. Some believe the angularity of traditional frame housing is sterile, pre-fabricated, less inviting and less comforting than the rounded corners of adobe. But to others, frame houses are resonant with their own childhood homes, and there is appeal in the clean, straight lines. [See Figure 2.2.]

Adobe houses with their imperfect lines and walls, with their curved-walled courtyards and flat roofs are really curvilinear—a marriage of male and female aspects. [See Figures 2:3 and 2:4.]

Figure 2:3 [above]
Exposed adobe wall enclosing main entrance to house.

Figure 2:4 [below]
Curvilinear courtyard walls in harmony with rounded Great Room of house.

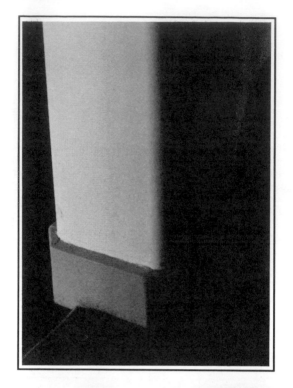

But, rounded walls and rounded corners can be included in frame houses at virtually no increase in cost. [See Figure 2.6.]

Deep window sills are natural in adobe houses and can be built easily by framing the house for them. [See Figure 2.6.]

How important is the look of hand-crafting, high-tech, or local, traditional architectural details? Our T.R.E.E. Homes, both adobe and frame, integrate traditional Southwest details into the functional aspects of the house. For example, exposed roof supports—vigas (peeled, unsawn logs used as support beams or posts) and roughcut planks (dimensioned lumber cut out of logs), or vigas and latillas (peeled or unpeeled branches or small trees)—are fully functional and traditional. We use corbels (short timbers placed under ceiling support beams to reduce their span and potential sagging) inside the house and on the portals. These personal choices can be built into your home at little or no extra cost when planned for in advance. [See Figures 2:7 and 2:8.]

Do you want wood-framed windows or will metal do? How important is graciousness? Or elegance? How do you relate to the earth itself, to gardening, to growing food for your own table? These issues impact on your plot of land, and your desires for landscaping and gardening affect the final decision—where to place the gardens in relation to the house—is this the best balance? [See Figure 2:9.]

Figure 2:5 [top left]
Interior frame wall with rounded edges.

Figure 2:6 [bottom left]
Deep window sills with roughcut frame.

Figure 2:7 [above]
Adobe accents around interior doorway.

Figure 2:8 [left]
Hand-troweled plaster banco around doorway.

Figure 2:9 [below]
Rock garden with low-care herbs in main courtyard near kitchen.

Figure 2:10 [above]
Talavera tiles on bath vanity.

How important is light, or coziness? What about fireplaces and rooms lined with books? Light implies windows, coziness implies fewer windows. A cozy library could be built on the north or west side where fewer windows are desirable from the standpoint of solar benefits. Don't be surprised if you need to make compromises. You may *want* a north window. Do it. You can save energy in other ways as you make choices in the building of your home.

Quality. A critical issue—quality of materials and workmanship. Our T.R.E.E. Homes are of the highest quality we can build. And your home should be the highest quality you can afford. This is a deep-seated belief. Buy the very best you can afford. You will not regret it. If a choice has to be made, build a smaller house, or do renovations one at a time, but use the highest quality materials that also satisfy your personal needs, and get the highest quality workmanship you can. Sometimes these choices do not cost more than standard practices; sometimes they cost only a little more, and sometimes they actually cost less. If you want a tile floor or tile counter tops, investigate local manufacturers or a warehouse store like HomeBase (currently in twelve states from Illinois to California) for recycled tiles. They exist. Or use air-dried (rather than kiln dried) tiles like Talavera or Saltillo from Mexico. Ask local masons, make choices. [See Figure 2:10.]

Do you want to keep the old trees, the native shrubs? Do you want to attract wildlife, have running water or a pond or grow herbs? Do you want to do something good for the environment—not just less damage? Retaining native and naturalized trees and shrubs (which can be done with foresight even when building from scratch) and planting trees helps counter the cutting of the trees that will provide lumber for your house.

Constructed wetlands can be built that actually are residential sewage treatment systems. These marshes and/or ponds can meet the desire for water areas and do something good and healthy for your immediate environment, too. These wetlands eliminate the possibility of ground water contamination from septic systems and will attract native wildlife to your yard. [See Figure 9:1.]

Is your lifestyle governed by career, family, a sense of global commitment, a hunger for harmony or spiritual connection? Any, or all, of these personal commitments can be met by designing and building, or renovating, your home with these personal criteria in mind. They will affect site location and orientation as well as the layout of the house, but they won't cost more if you integrate them from the beginning. ∎

# 3 CHAPTER

## REPAIR WHAT EXISTS Live A Better way

The simplest way to begin is to start with what we already have. Whatever we do to make our homes better will benefit us in the short term and all of us in the long term. In addition, many of the maintenance projects and landscaping projects suggested in this book will make houses more saleable. They don't just help the environment, they become added value, true home improvements. Areas we discuss will include:

- Repairs/Maintenance
- Recycling
- Finishes
- Appliances
- Overhangs/Awnings
- Landscaping

### REPAIRS/MAINTENANCE

Maintenance is a key factor. The more we keep things in good working order, the more serviceable we design them, the longer they will last, and the more efficiently they will perform. We will get more for our money and will do less damage to the environment by not having to replace things sooner than necessary. There is no need to spend enormous amounts of money or add spaces or replace everything at once to improve your home and make it more harmonious with the natural environment. When something needs fixing or replacing, make a choice.

Caulk around the windows and doors. Weatherstrip where necessary. Nearly one-half of all energy used in our homes is wasted. It simply leaks out. Keep your furnace and evaporative cooler in good repair. Tune up your furnace; have it cleaned and adjusted periodically. Clean and replace filters in your dryer, furnace, air conditioner or evaporative cooler. The appliances will work better and use less energy. They will also last longer. Keep your basic systems—plumbing, electricity, gas—in good working order. The better you maintain them, the more efficiently, and better, they work. Not only will they last longer, they will use much less energy in the short term, and you will prevent future problems.

*Nearly one-half of all energy used in our homes is wasted. It simply leaks out.*

## RECYCLING

As we said earlier, recycling should become our first question. Can we buy recycled products, and how do we recycle products we are through with? Recycling has become relatively easy and, as time goes on, will probably become much more prevalent than it is today. Most of us can easily recycle newspapers (by 1988 approximately 29% of newspapers were being recycled), glass, aluminum, plastic, tin, corrugated paper, and more.

Check with local services and centers for their requirements. Even local businesses often have huge dumpsters set up for drop-off recycling.

## FINISHES

Not every surface needs to be finished. Some woods weather beautifully without our help—like rough pine plank fences—and many of the products used for sealing and finishing are hazardous—in production, in application, and in disposal.

If sealers are needed, you can buy the base ingredients and mix what you need—at much less cost. You can re-strain and re-use these products (such as mineral spirits), and when you're done, let them evaporate rather than dumping them in landfills.

The San Francisco Household Hazardous Waste Facility estimated that paint and paint products (oil-based paint, thinners, solvents, stains and finishes) accounted for 60% of hazardous waste dumped by individuals, so painting is a big issue. Whitewash is an alternative to paint. Latex paint is overall less hazardous than oil-based paint—to use and to get rid of. Oil-based paint pigments are often made with heavy metals such as cadmium and titanium dioxide which make cleaning up and disposing of left-overs dangerous. The heavy metals seep into the ground and lead to groundwater pollution, contaminating our drinking water. And they could evaporate, contaminating the air. However, oil-based paints are more durable. Rather than throw paint away, use it as the primer base-coat for a new paint job, or donate it to a school or a senior center. Wood stains without naptha should be used if staining is necessary.

When we seal exposed wood, inside and outside of the house, we use an exterior wood preservative. In wet climates this is even more important than it is here in the high desert of New Mexico. This contributes to longer lasting wood elements and reduces the possibility of insect (termite) infestations not only to the wood itself but to the interior of the house and its framing. In addition, the sealer makes the wood look more "finished." Cedar and redwood can be used, untreated, for trim as it weathers naturally and well, or oils such as tung or linseed can be applied.

Sealers on brick floors are necessary to protect the floors from use and to discourage insect infestations. Customers also like the shiny surface sealers provide on brick floors. There are few great choices here—the good sealers also have hazardous properties.

One of the best, a finish used on gym floors, is oil-based and uses VOCs (volatile organic compounds—hydrocarbons and solvents) as the carrier for polyurethane. Noxious odors are released during application also, making it a low-level hazardous product to use. Outgassing (the leaching of vapors after application to the surface) occurs during drying, but ultimately dry, hard, polyurethane is left. Water-based sealers do exist, but they often cost four times as much, increasing the average cost of a house by approximately $3,000—a significant price.

## APPLIANCES

Maintain your appliances—from draining the sediments from your hot water heater periodically, to changing the filters in your furnaces and air conditioners. Maintain proper air and/or water flow to your appliances—keep air intakes free of brush and other dry growth, and make sure furnace rooms vent adequately to the outside.

With current technology, gas appliances seem preferable to electric ones—certainly for hot water heaters, ranges, and dryers. Gas furnaces in cold weather climates are significantly less costly to run. And gas pollutes the environment less than coal-burning utilities that provide many of us with electricity. If buying a new gas range, get one with electronic ignition. It uses approximately 40% less gas than one with a pilot light.

Using aerators on faucets reduces the amount of water used at any given time, but does not reduce its effectiveness. Substitute "Low-Flo" shower heads and make your toilet a water saver (e.g. displace some water in the tank with a re-cycled plastic bottle already full of water).

Long-lasting light bulbs, and domestic fluorescent bulbs are becoming more widely available. They will save money over the long haul as they are far more efficient in their use of energy.

Ask questions of dealers, service centers, manufacturers. Read books and magazines that compare brands with "state of the art" technology.

Figure 3:1 [above]
Overhang at appropriate height to allow winter sun to shine into windows.

## OVERHANGS/AWNINGS

Solar power (passive or active) has become an integral part of many homes. Our T.R.E.E Home assumes use of passive solar techniques. In hot, sunny climates, however, solar power needs to be deflected in the summertime. Cooling shade becomes equally important. Sunlight warming a brick floor will warm the air surrounding it, whether in summer or winter. Too much sun in the summer wastes air conditioning, making our appliances work harder than necessary. And we waste money, spending more on utility bills than we need to.

On our passive solar homes we build over-hangs above the windows. They act as awnings during the summer and do not interfere with the desirable winter sun. [See Figures 3:1 and 3:2.]

Figure 3:2 [right]
Overhangs / "Eyebrows" for summer shade.

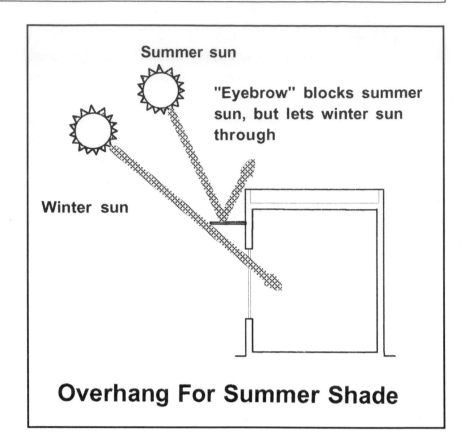

Figure 3:3 [right]
Overhang for summer shade.

The angle of the winter sun is lower than the summer angle; therefore, with the correct placement of the overhangs, the summer sun is deflected but the winter sun is not. [See Figure 3:3.]

This process can be effected with awnings, or portals (porches), or even with landscaping—planting a deciduous shade tree. [See Figures 4:6, 4:7, 4:8.] For specific technical data, refer to *The Passive Solar Energy Book* by Edward Mazria (See Bibliography).

The overhangs, as well as porch posts and roof decking, are built with roughcut lumber which is not kiln dried or surfaced. The use of roughcut saves considerable energy and waste. A planed 2" x 4" measures 1.5" x 3.5", which wastes the rough edges. It is more processed (using more energy), and is not made locally in the Southwest, which increases shipping costs.

| FIGURE 3:4   **LUMBER COMPARISON** | | |
| --- | --- | --- |
| MATERIAL | ENERGY CONSUMPTION | % COMPARISON |
| Roughcut | 145 kw/ 1000 bdft | 100% |
| Surfaced lumber | 3048 kw/ 1000 bdft | 2102% |
| Plywood | 4358 kw/ 1000 bdft | 3006% |
| | kw  = kilowatt hours | |
| | bdft = board feet | |

## LANDSCAPING

Plant a tree. That refrain seems to be everywhere. It's a reaction to the reduction of the forests, to the destruction of the rain forests, and it's simple to do. When placed appropriately, planting a deciduous tree can shade a sunny window in the summer and its bare branches allow the sun in during the colder winter months. A fruit tree will contribute to your pantry

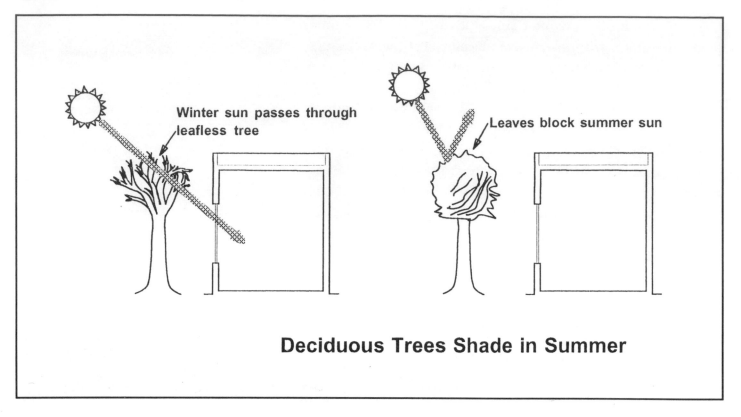

Winter sun passes through leafless tree

Leaves block summer sun

**Deciduous Trees Shade in Summer**

Figure 3:5 [above]
Deciduous trees shade in summer.

and perhaps reduce your grocery bill. [See Figures 3:5 and 3:6.]

Planting drought-tolerant grass will reduce your use of water and keep the air cooler around your house during the summer. Here in the high desert of the American Southwest, xeriscape (landscaping designed to survive without adding water or fertilizer, using native plantings) is gaining ground. Following its precepts will save precious water and maintain a solid ecological balance with nature.

Do what is natural in your area. It is an easy, effective way to landscape. Find out about indigenous grasses that need little care, that thrive in your soil. Watering grass not suited to dry climates is wasteful, and using fertilizer pollutes the ground and the water. Native grasses need less water and often need no fertilizers or chemical enhancers. The use of native shrubs and trees tend to make for a healthier garden and may attract native wildlife, like birds and butterflies, keeping your own yard's eco-system in healthy balance. [See Figure 3:7.] ■

Figure 3:6 [above]
Deciduous apple trees allow sun to shine
through in winter. [See Figure 8:4 for
summer view of same orchard.]

Figure 3:7 [left]
Native and naturalized plantings: Russian
Olives and Fourwing Saltbush.

# 4 CHAPTER

## BUILDING NEW Starting From Scratch

Many people build, or have built, their own homes, so they get exactly what they want and need: a house that delivers on aesthetics, individual spaces, and how they want to live. You can compromise less when you start from scratch. Renovations, as we've discussed, must take into account what is already there—if you have a flat roof, it is more difficult and more expensive to make it a pitched roof. Adding-on is somewhat like renovating in that most people try to add on in unobtrusive ways, attempting to stay within the style of the original building. But starting from scratch allows you to do exactly what you want, from an environmental standpoint as well as aesthetic. And while custom building is often more expensive than buying something already built, it is not necessarily more expensive than buying a "fixer-upper" and renovating.

In Chapters 4 and 5 we discuss those aspects of building that we believe impact the environment, and make recommendations we have developed over the years that minimize the negative effects on the environment. We conducted a study that analyzed many of these important criteria and we have continued to refine our recommendations based on new information and new products.

We will not go into construction detail about every aspect of building a house. There are many books available that cover those subjects. [See the Bibliography for a partial list.]

Our Timber Reduced Energy Efficient homes are of the

highest possible quality; they integrate products and techniques that are sensitive to the environment, and they are relatively easy and inexpensive to maintain. Importantly, while our homes are "custom built," they are competitive in price to the general housing market. Our homes minimize their impact on the environment both in terms of construction and in terms of living in them. This does not mean they have "no impact" on the environment—that would be impossible—but it does mean we do everything possible to ensure we end up with the highest quality homes that do the least possible damage. Our recommendations take into account the energy required to obtain, manufacture, ship and install various building materials. We consider the size and kind of tree required to make the various wooden components, and we assess the heating, cooling, and other operational costs of the on-going running of the home. We recycle as we build, and we use the least toxic materials available that meet the requirements of the specific job. And we are always looking for ways to improve what we do.

Our adobe houses and our frame houses are virtually identical, in terms of building materials and techniques, except for the exterior walls. The foundation, the roof system, the interior walls, and the garage are the same. The foundation of an adobe house will be wider, but only because adobe walls are wider than frame ones. The interior walls and the garage are all of frame construction. Vigas, corbels, and Southwest accents (rounded corners, exposed wood, interior exposed adobe walls) are also the same for either type house. Porches, portals, doors, and windows—all are built the same. [See Chapter 8 for photos and details of similar adobe and frame T.R.E.E. homes.]

The exterior walls, however, are different. Adobe houses have adobe walls, sheathed on the outside with rigid insulation, then stuccoed, and painted or plastered on the inside. Frame walls are sheathed on the outside with rigid insulation, then stuccoed, and sheathed on the inside with gypsum board, then painted. The frame cavity is also filled with insulation. These processes are discussed more fully in Chapter 5.


SITE SELECTION AND ORIENTATION

Site selection is extremely personal. Buying the land in

volves money, time, and all kinds of rational considerations—how expensive will it be to get water, utilities, deliveries? Do we have to build our own road, or are we already in a developed area? But most of all, site selection is emotional. Is this the piece of land I want? Can I breathe freely? Is there a view? Are my neighbors too close, or too far away? How do I/we feel about this place? It will probably have to be a compromise. You will look at places in reasonable commuting distance to your work, in reasonable proximity to good schools for your children, but with the amenities you want—near water or with a great view. It's your choice. Whatever you choose, it is simply your first choice, among hundreds to come. [See Figures 4:1 and 4:2.]

With house orientation, once you've built your house, it's done. It is a basic decision. You can always change a door you

Figure 4:1 [above]
House oriented toward Sandia Mountains.

Figure 4:2 [facing page]
House oriented toward country lane and city of Albuquerque.

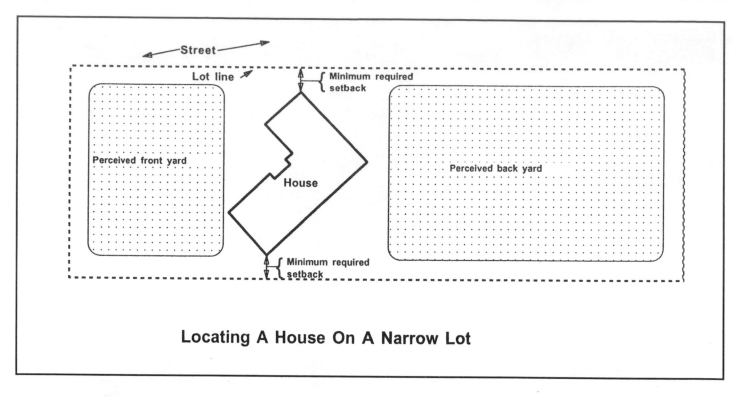

**Locating A House On A Narrow Lot**

Figure 4:3 [above]
Locating a house on a narrow lot.

Figure 4:4 [below]
Ideal floor plan for solar orientation.

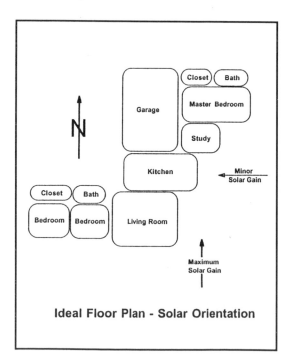

**Ideal Floor Plan - Solar Orientation**

don't like, or the hardware. But if the site is wrong, you have to move. And once the house is built, it is very difficult to re-orient the basic layout. [See Figure 4:5 and Chapter 8 for more examples.]

Feel your way into this area. Take into account all the rational pros and cons; read books about Feng Shui, the Chinese art of placement. An example: if you live in hilly country, a south facing slope is preferable from the standpoint of heating and cooling (the north-facing slope is cooler, requiring more heat in the winter.) Be prepared for what your site may contribute to the ultimate cost of your home. If you choose a site near the river, chances are your well will not have to be very deep, but if you choose to live up on a hilltop your well might have to be 700 feet deep, and drilling a well may be one of the bigger initial expenses in the building of your home. [See Figure 4:3.]

Our T.R.E.E. home concept integrates passive solar design into the overall plans for the house, so orientation is a primary consideration when starting the plan. The rooms with the least use—garages, store rooms, etc.—may be set on the north side of the house, while the rooms with greatest use, living rooms and bed-rooms, may be set on the south to take advantage of solar heat-ing and cooling. Orienting the house helps determine where the windows will be and in which rooms. We attempt to maximize the use of windows on the east and south, minimizing windows on the west and north. Orientation also deter-

Figure 4:5 [above]
Sweeping views East and South with southern exposure for trombe wall.

mines where the driveway will be, how the entrance will be devised, and how to deal with street-side issues of privacy. [See Figure 4:4.]

Orientation also helps determine major landscaping issues early-on. For example: are trees already present? Where should we plant trees to effectively shade windows and roofs? But orientation is also an emotional, aesthetic issue. Where are the views; what do you want to see from your bedroom, the kitchen, the living room? Decide what you want, up front, and you can compensate if your orientation ends up being less than perfectly solar-efficient. [See Figure 4:5.]

## SOLAR ENERGY

Solar energy is a massive subject, so we are not going to try to cover all aspects of the subject here. There are many books already written on this subject. Edward Mizria, for example, has written what many consider to be the "bible" of solar energy, *The Passive Solar Energy Book*. What is important here, is being aware of what we can do, easily, to benefit from solar energy, and how to find out what to do next.

We build passive solar homes, designed to obtain direct solar gain, mostly for heating and cooling the house. We are not

Figure 4:8 [above]
North facing portal protects front entry.

Figure 4:6 [below]  East facing portal.

going to address active solar energy (except in a later chapter when we speculate about the future), nor will we go into technical detail about angles of the sun and deflection.

Site selection, orientation, windows, walls, floors, portals, landscaping, skylights—all affect how much benefit we will obtain from solar power. If we build on the north slope of a hill we will get less than if we face south. We will gain more from solar power if we have big windows, and more of them, on the east and south sides of our house and fewer, small ones on the north and west. Trombe walls (adobe walls on the south facing exterior, often covered with non-vented glass to retain heat gathered during the day) that absorb and radiate heat on the south side can supply virtually all the heat a house needs, but, as we said previously, a well-insulated house does the job even better. A masonry, earth, or brick floor can absorb and radiate heat gained from direct sunlight. Properly designed porches or portals can provide needed shade during the summer months, as can deciduous shade trees, and not interfere severely with the desired warmth of the winter sun. Skylights bring free light indoors. No house should be built without due consideration given to solar orientation and its benefits.

## PORCHES/ PORTALS

Porches and portals would be built only on the east side of a "pure" solar house. [See Figure 4:6.]

The north side is too cold; the south gets too much sun, and on the west the sun would radiate the heat under the porch as it sets. Overhangs are built to shade sun-facing windows from the high, hot summer sun. However, extenuating circumstances could alter your choices. For example, if you have a stand of shade trees on the west, a portal could function very well. [See Figure 4:7.]

Or you may want a portal protecting an outside door, no matter which direction it faces, even North. [See Figure 4:8.]

We use roughcut lumber for the support posts and decking of our portals, just as we do for our interior ceilings. It suits our homes aesthetically and is far cheaper to use, both in terms of actual cost as well as the fact that it is available locally. We also use corbels to reduce the span of the long support beams. We make the corbels, often, out of 2" x 6"s, which also reduces our use of large dimensioned lumber. [See Figure 4:9.]

Figure 4:7 [above]
West portal shaded by tall cottonwood trees.

Figure 4:9 [below]
Portal post and corbel.

*A well-insulated,
well-built house
saves many thousands
of dollars in energy use
over the life of the house.*

INSULATION

We use insulation to ensure an energy efficient house. A well-insulated, well-built house saves many thousands of dollars in energy use over the life of the house. It retains heat and cool air effectively. Insulation also provides a sound barrier and fire protection.

In the exterior wall cavities of a frame house, between the ceiling and the roof, and in interior wall cavities between living, bedroom, and bath areas, we use cellulose insulation impregnated with borate. Cellulose is recycled newspapers (and newspapers represent a major percentage of slow-decomposing waste in landfills). This insulation is inexpensive, long-lasting, not harmful to humans, resistant to fire and insect infestation (termites), and borate is a wood preservative that protects against mold and mildew. Cellulose does what we want it to do.

We use rigid insulation on the outside walls—down to the base of the foundation footings—on both our frame and adobe houses. It is still the best option considering the effectiveness of the product, its ease of handling, and its cost. We use grayboard rigid insulation less now than we have in the past. Even though we realize this is probably the most harmful material we use in building—in terms of the environment—we are constantly looking for other alternatives. Polystyrene contributes to pollution during manufacture, but it is far down the scale. Cars and cows contribute far more to this problem than polystyrene. One alternative would be to not insulate the house as completely as we do, but the increase in heating and cooling costs creates much more pollution. However, we continue to look for improved ways to reduce our use of polystyrene, both by using products with less CFCs and/or HCFCs and by encouraging manufacturers to make the product without CFCs altogether.

Our use of polystyrene rigid insulation is an example of how we make our choices, and how we move toward using less and less hazardous materials all the time. We started out using poly-iso rigid insulation in the ceilings as well as in the walls of our homes. After analyzing insulation as part of our ongoing assessment process and finding out that ISO was expensive energy-wise and damaging to the ozone, we started using cellulose in the ceilings (and inside the wall cavities of our frame houses) while using grayboard (made with less damaging HCFCs) as our exterior rigid insulation/outer sheathing. We now use cellulose in as many places as we can and are in the process of exploring the possibilities of rigid cellulose sheathing.

ISO (polyisocyanurate) is still widely used and is made with CFC-11, which eventually leaks out into the atmosphere. ISO is 10-15% CFCs. Grayboard (extruded polystyrene) is the rigid insulation of choice for below-grade (below ground) use and is used for wall sheathing, too. Originally made with methyl chloride, in the 1960s manufacturers exchanged that agent for CFC-12. By the late 1980s, most manufacturers began switching to HCFC-142b and ethyl chloride, which is estimated to deplete the ozone far less (its potential is approximately 94% less) than CFC-12. But, HCFCs are also deleterious to the ozone, contribute to global warming, and actually break down faster than CFCs.

The only rigid insulations available that are not made with CFCs or HCFCs are fiberglass and EPS (expanded polystyrene, also known as beadboard). EPS is made using pentane as the foaming agent. The fiberglass product is not widely available for residential use and needs cladding (covering) for below-grade use. For a long time, EPS was not considered to be of high enough quality because of its lower R values (figures used to

FIGURE 4:10   **INSULATION COMPARISON**

| | R-30 ROOF | | PERV | DISADVANTAGES |
|---|---|---|---|---|
| | Inches of Material | Energy (kwh) | (kwh/1000 sqft/ R-Val) | |
| Polyiso | 4.8 | 432 | 14.4 | CFCs + other hazardous chemicals |
| Glass fiber | 9.2 | 566 | 18.8 | High energy use, pollution, hazardous to work with |
| Foamed glass | 10.5 | 792 | 26.4 | Pollution, high price |
| Polystyrene | 6.9 | 1058 | 35.3 | Use limited resources, high energy use, pollution, combustible |
| Expanded Perlite | 9.6 | 879 * | 29.3 * | High energy use, use of limited resources, open pit mines, difficult to use |
| Cellulose | 7.7 | 87 | 2.9 | Use of limited resource, mining suspect, not in rigid form, needs knowledgeable installer |

* Energy numbers do not include mining, crushing, sizing.
Source:  Aiming for the T.R.E.E. House 11/89

Figure 4:11 [above]
Interior sandwich design door. Front view.

Figure 4:12 [below]
Interior sandwich design door. Edge view.

measure a material's resistance to heat flow—the higher the R- value the better its insulating properties) and lower structural integrity. We believe it is now made in higher densities that are satisfactory for both above and below-grade use. However, it is not yet readily nor easily available.

Our assessment of this situation leads us to use grayboard for below-grade use, and styrofoam for exterior wall sheathing, above-grade. It is not a perfect solution, but a balanced one.

Chart 4:10 [on preceeding page] compares some standard insulation choices based on providing roof insulation of R-30. Today, we insulate the roofs of our T.R.E.E. homes to a level of R-50. The study from which these figures are cited was done before EPS (a high density rigid insulation that does not incorporate CFCs or HCFCs) was widely available. Our use of cellulose, wherever we can, is justified by its low PERV (Processing Energy to R-Value Ratio) as shown below. We are developing Cellusheathing™ [patent pending], cellulose manufactured into a rigid form—maybe via recycled cardboard (essentially expanded and filled with cellulose). [See Figure 4:10.]

We insulate our T.R.E.E. homes so well that trombe walls are no longer cost effective. [See Chapter 5 on walls.] Our use of cellulose and rigid insulation allows us to build any kind of house a client wants, efficiently. And it will be a low cost house to maintain.

## DOORS AND WINDOWS

The placement of exterior doors and windows bears some thought right from the beginning. Doors determine traffic paths, the manner of exiting and arriving. Windows affect what views are seen from which rooms, affect energy loss and gain, and the amount of privacy or openness a room has. Both windows and doors will affect energy efficiency, security, and aesthetic impressions of the house. Doors with glass and windows on the east and south are fine. No or few, windows on the north and

Figure 4:13 [above right]
Frame wall with burglar blocks

Figure 4:14 [below right]
Exterior solid wood door.

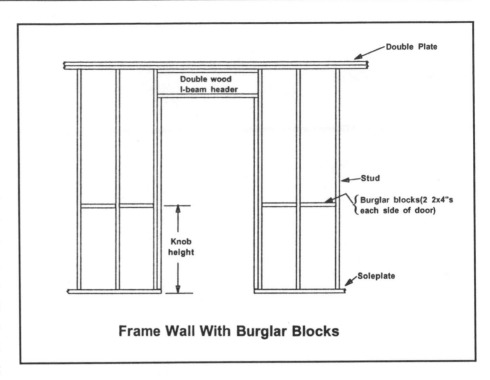

**Frame Wall With Burglar Blocks**

solid doors will minimize heat loss in the colder months.

We prefer interior doors that are hand-made, of locally manufactured roughcut lumber, of a sandwich design with opposing grain layers and wood pegs, which keeps the doors straight and true. A little design effort has proved a good investment, for greater durability and reduction of noise. When doors last longer, they are less wasteful. Hollow core doors, which are widely used, do not inhibit sound, and look sterile. [See Figures 4:11 and 4:12.]

Exterior door frames include wood blocking at door handle height, increasing the rigidity of the wall. This bracing makes the door much less susceptible to break-ins. Usually, burglars spread the door jamb away from the lock bolt, but the wood blocking makes this virtually impossible. [See Figure 4:13.]

We use manufactured exterior doors. The best doors are insulated steel, but most people want wood, and the manufactured ones are strong and well sealed. [See Figure 4:14.]

Double paned glass, metal framed windows with thermal breaks are our recommended window. They will last for thirty years or more and are virtually maintenance free. Traditionally, windows were made of wood and glass and we earlier moved away from wood for easier maintenance. But, now, people again want wood, for its beauty. So wood windows are the popular choice—many people like the look of the wood and are willing to care for it. Our second choice is metal clad (metal on the outside, wood on the inside) windows so the wood is there for its beauty, but not on the outside where it will weather—rot, crack, shrink, or expand. Appraisers take

Figure 4:15 [above left]
Aluminum windows.

Figure 4:16 [above right]
Rounded frame wall near exterior door.

points off for wood windows today for just these reasons. They do not wear as well. [See Figure 4:15.]

We do not usually recommend triple glass. It seems to be overkill. And we recommend low E glass only for those areas where the sun will seriously fade rugs and furniture. Low E stands for low-emissivity, the property of a material that reflects the long-wave infrared energy, increasing the insulating properties of the material it is next to and reducing the fading/ deteriorating qualities of the light. One of the drawbacks of direct solar gain is the potential for damaging furniture and rugs from the sun's light and heat.

Glass itself is not a "free" material—it causes pollution in its manufacturing process and is hazardous because of its "fibers," which can be inhaled. But there are no adequate alternatives to glass at this time.

We round the edges of the walls near the doors and windows with metal bullnose strips on our Southwest style frame houses, so all edges of the house, whether created by walls, doors, or windows are softly rounded. [See Figures 4:16 and 4:17.]

Of course, the edges of the adobe walls near doors and windows are naturally rounded. [See Figure 4:18.]

## TYPES OF BUILDING

The T.R.E.E. home concept has been developed specifical-

ly for the building of adobe homes and standard frame homes. We are now in the process of building a tire house, which will utilize used tires as the basic material for the exterior walls. [See Chapter 7.] And, right now, the tires are free. However, the techniques and products recommended for our frame or adobe houses can be integrated into many different types of buildings—masonry (of which adobe is one kind), log, etc. The choice of building material is in part determined by local codes and regulations as well as by the climatic conditions of your building site. Adobe is a good material for the Southwest with its extremes of hot and cold in a given 24 hour period, but it is not such an ideal material in climates that are more even throughout the day and night. (This is in part due to the heat retaining/cooling properties of adobe mass—warming the house inside during the night while the cold night air cools the house, so it stays cooler during the following day.) Where the climate is more equally cool or warm during 24 hours, the mass of the adobe does not have the opportunity to cool and warm in alternating cycles.

This book is not about what specific materials to use, but we will point out the qualities of construction that contribute to the desired end result—temperature control, insulation, or quiet—that can be built into any type of house you decide to build. ∎

Figure 4:17 [above left]
Rounded exterior frame wall near window.

Figure 4:18 [above right]
Window in adobe wall.

# 5 CHAPTER

# FRAME AND ADOBE Foundations, Walls, Floors and Roofs

The foundation, walls, floor, and roof are the "body" of a house, and it is here we have developed techniques that most significantly reduce our impact on the environment. We have designed building units and processes that use smaller logs, scrap lumber, and reduce the use of concrete in our adobe houses.

## FOUNDATIONS

The foundation supports the house with all of its dead (the house and appliances) and live (people, furniture, rain and wind) weight. The foundation consists of three main parts: the bed (the earth); the footing; and the foundation wall (the structural part). Foundations can be built with continuous footings or on piers, but essentially the three sections serve the same purpose—to ensure stability. The earth must be as stable as possible, the footing sits on the stabilized earth and supports the wall, which distributes the weight of the building. The footings are usually wider, deeper, than the wall.

The choice of foundation is based on the kind and size of house you will build above it and on the site you've chosen. Climatic conditions are important, as is the content of the earth beneath the foundation (clay vs sand), the depth of the water table, and the drainage properties of the site. Codes and regulations must also be taken into account.

For example, the American Southwest is hot and arid, and in many places subject to high winds, whereas in Florida, the climate is humid, the land can be swampy and weather patterns include hurricanes and other massive tropical storms. The houses and the stresses they will be subject to are very different, so ask local experts, and look to indigenous method—what buildings are still standing after hundreds of years—to see what works.

Since most of the United States is subject to frost, foundations must be built to withstand the pressures of freezing and warming, and in most places the foundations must be set below the frost line. Frost can heave footings and damage the superstructure. Footings must be of non-absorbent, closed-cell materials. And they must be moisture resistant.

So, the foundation, at minimum, must: have strength (to support the walls and weight of the building); not be sensitive to freezing (freezing will damage the entire structure); and be set below the frost line and insulated against heat loss.

The key to an efficient foundation is to avoid structural failure without extravagant waste. The T.R.E.E. home foundation has footings built on compacted, undisturbed earth (most solid, most compact ground). We use concrete footings, larger than specified by code to ensure no foundation shift. We embed steel rebar in the concrete for additional strength. We insulate the foundation at least 24" deep all the way to the bottoms of the footings. The insulation is 1.5" thick and has an R-value of 7.5, again, above code. We have been using closed- cell polystyrene to ensure no water absorption. [Beware of white-colored insulation as it is of open-cell design and can absorb water which greatly reduces its insulating properties.] The insulated foundation makes the house more energy efficient in the long run, as it reduces the absorption of cold from the earth. Placing the insulation on the outside of the foundation allows us to take advantage of the thermal mass properties of the wall (whatever the material). Reduction of water absorption is important also, to minimize the possibility of freezing as well as moisture penetration into the building itself. [See Figures 5:1 and 5:2.]

The foundations are identical in design, technique, and materials for both our adobe and frame houses. The adobe house foundations are wider because the adobe walls are wider.

*The key to an efficient foundation is to avoid structural failure without extravagant waste.*

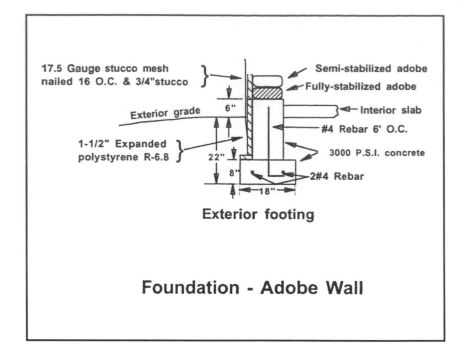

**Foundation - Adobe Wall**

Figure 5:1 [top right]
Adobe wall foundation.

Figure 5:2 [bottom right]
Frame wall foundation.

Figure 5:3 [below]
Foundation trench for frame house.

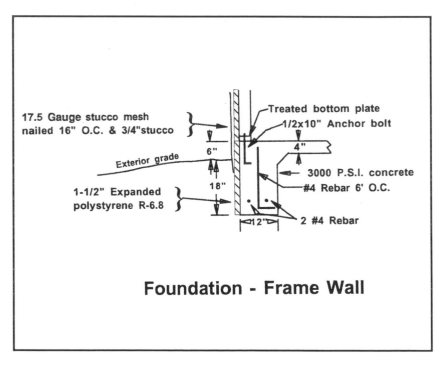

**Foundation - Frame Wall**

Concrete is not an ideal material. It is energy intensive to produce (Cement = 1274 kwh/ 1000 cu. ft.) and it causes substantial pollution: carbon oxides, sulfur oxides, acids, chrome components, and enormous dust. The use of reinforcing steel adds considerably to the energy consumed in the building of the house. However, we know of no good alternatives. [See Figure 5:3.]

WALLS

The walls are the basic structural frame of the house. They form its shape and determine its primary strength. It is easiest to think of walls as having three basic aspects: outside, inside, and the cavity of the wall itself. Originally, walls were very simple structures made to protect us from our enemies. They were upright, plain walls. Now, however, we use them to support other structures, like a roof system, and we punch holes in them for windows and doors, reducing their natural integrity and strength. Walls must have strength, durability, and, they must allow and account for insulation.

Walls must have load bearing (compressive) strength to hold up the roof and racking (ability to withstand the pressure to go "out of square") strength; they must be resistant to weathering, chemical degradation, and atmospheric pollution. They must have low combustibility, be resistant to impact, withstand dimensional changes due to temperature and moisture, and be resistant to insect attacks and moisture penetration. Walls control the flow of heat, moisture, air, and sound.

The durability of a wall is more dependent on heat flow, temperature changes, and moisture absorption than any other factors. Moisture from within a wall is even worse, more damaging, than external moisture. Condensation in walls wets the structural materials as well as the insulation and reduces the insulating qualities of both.

The only place our adobe homes differ from our frame homes is in the construction of the exterior walls. Therefore, in this section, we discuss adobe exterior walls and frame exterior walls indepently.

ADOBE HOUSE WALLS

The adobes themselves are the inner cavity in an adobe house and we use both fully-stabilized and semi-stabilized adobes, containing asphalt emulsion for water resistance. The fully stabilized adobes are used as the first layer of adobe above the foundation. You can make your own adobes by hand, by yourself, or you can buy them commercially. [See Figure 5:4.]

To strengthen our adobe walls, we use ladder-type steel reinforcement in the mud joints, every two feet vertically through-

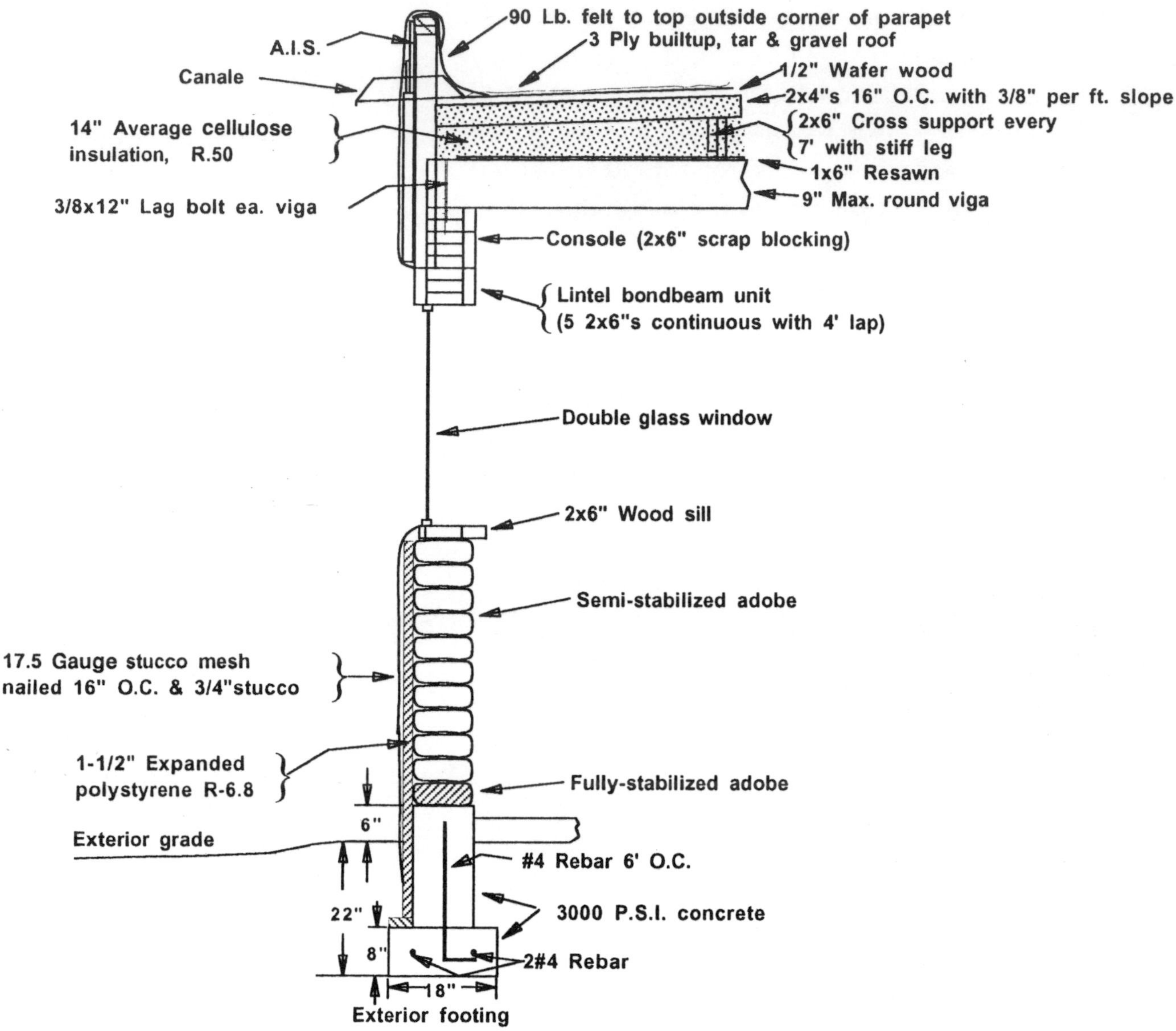
A.I.S.
Canale
14" Average cellulose insulation, R.50
3/8x12" Lag bolt ea. viga
90 Lb. felt to top outside corner of parapet
3 Ply builtup, tar & gravel roof
1/2" Wafer wood
2x4"s 16" O.C. with 3/8" per ft. slope
2x6" Cross support every 7' with stiff leg
1x6" Resawn
9" Max. round viga
Console (2x6" scrap blocking)
Lintel bondbeam unit (5 2x6"s continuous with 4' lap)
Double glass window
2x6" Wood sill
Semi-stabilized adobe
17.5 Gauge stucco mesh nailed 16" O.C. & 3/4"stucco
1-1/2" Expanded polystyrene R-6.8
Fully-stabilized adobe
6"
Exterior grade
#4 Rebar 6' O.C.
22"
3000 P.S.I. concrete
8"
2#4 Rebar
18"
Exterior footing

## Adobe Wall Cross Section

out the entire wall. At every window and door jamb, the steel is bent vertically 2" and stapled to the jamb. The 1.5" barbed fence staples effectively attach the window and door jambs to the adobe wall, adding vertical strength, which it was lacking. This method is simpler, easier, and faster than using the more traditional "gringo blocks" or other methods to install windows and doors. [See Figure 5.5.]

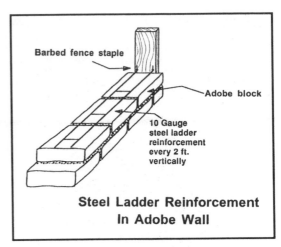

**Steel Ladder Reinforcement In Adobe Wall**

Figure 5:5 [above]
Steel ladder reinforcement
in adobe wall.

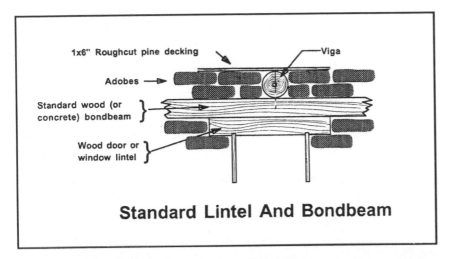

**Standard Lintel And Bondbeam**

Figure 5:6 [top left]
Standard lintel and bondbeam.

Figure 5:7 [bottom left]
Standard lintel and bondbeam.

As we discussed before, adobe walls often have openings in them. A lintel (a horizontal member spanning an opening to carry a superstructure) is used above each opening to maintain the wall's strength. At the top of an adobe wall (or any masonry wall) a bondbeam (a beam of either wood or cement, laid along the top of the adobe wall to support the ceiling beams) is built to spread the weight of the superstructure across the adobe wall. [See Figures 5:6 and 5:7.]

Figure 5:4 [facing page]
Adobe wall cross section.

Figure 5:8 [above]
LBU: Lintel bondbeam unit.

Figure 5:9 [below]
LBU: Lintel bondbeam unit

We began building adobe houses in the standard way, using cement bondbeams and lintels as large as 8" x 12", requiring the cutting of large, old trees. We developed an alternative—the LBU (the Lintel Bondbeam Unit). It makes the lintel and the bondbeam one piece. We designed the LBU to use lumber of smaller dimensions and discovered that we could even use wood that had crooked edges or still retained some bark. These imperfections are allowable, as part of the LBU is ultimately hidden in the wall. The basic idea is to substitute the lintel—a monolithic piece of lumber—with a stack of 2" thick boards. This system uses the plywood effect—opposing grains in connected layers of wood, increasing the strength of the final unit. [See Figures 5:8 and 5:9]

Using 2" boards, or even 4" or 6", requires smaller (younger) trees than using an 8" or 12" piece of lumber. We also are able to eliminate the use of concrete as the bondbeam, which, as we've already discussed, is one of our goals.

As the chart on page 59 shows, the LBU actually uses more lumber but less energy. The lumber used, however, is of smaller dimension and some is often considered scrap.

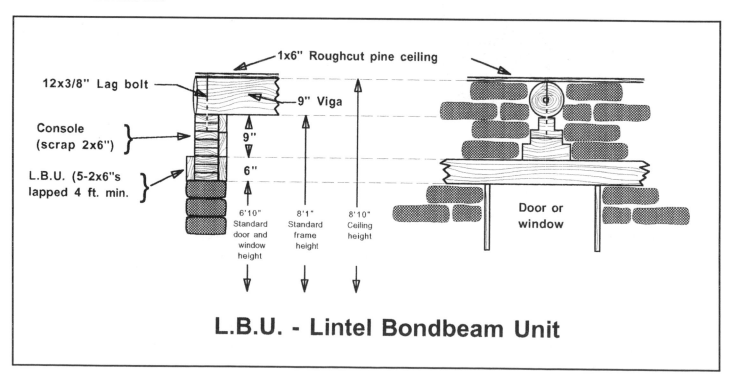

## L.B.U. - Lintel Bondbeam Unit

FIGURE 5: 10    **LINTEL/BONDBEAM COMPARISONS**

|  | Standard Lintel/Bondbeam | LBU - Lintel BondbeamUnit | STANDARD/LBU Comparison |
|---|---|---|---|
| Bdft | 1300 | 1729 | 133% |
| Kwh | 398 | 251 | 63 |
| Acres harvested | .5 | .6 |  |

Figure 5:11 [above]
Console in adobe wall.

Consoles are also made of small-dimensioned timber. They are wood blocks stacked under the vigas (or other ceiling support beams) to raise the height of the roof structure. In addition, they are an aesthetically pleasing design element. [See Figue 5:11.]

Inside our adobe homes, the adobes are sealed before being painted. The sealer acts as a bonding agent with the paint, preventing chipping. When a sheetrock wall (from an interior frame wall) adjoins an adobe wall, we cut a groove in the adobe to ensure a crack-free union.

A 10" standard adobe wall has an R-Value of 4.0, which, in our opinion, is no longer adequate to achieve significant reductions in the costs associated with heating and cooling the house. Therefore, we apply rigid insulation to the outside of our adobe houses, bringing the R-Value of the wall up to R-14. The R-14 adobe-walled house has a greater thermal mass than a frame house with R-22 walls, and the utility bills of similar size houses are virtually identical. [See Chapter 8 for details on similar houses and Chapter 4 on insulation options.]

Trombe walls are no longer cost effective either. A trombe wall, with an R-value of 4-6, is really a heat source. It is builtwith 10" of adobe on the inside, 4" of air space, and sealed with double pane glass on the outside. With our well-insulated houses, that deliver more than R-14 in the walls, a trombe wall that delivers R-6 simply is not good enough. So, the choice of adobe becomes, increasingly, an aesthetic decision not a solar/ energy one. [See Figue 5:12.]

Figure 5:12 [below]
Trombe wall.

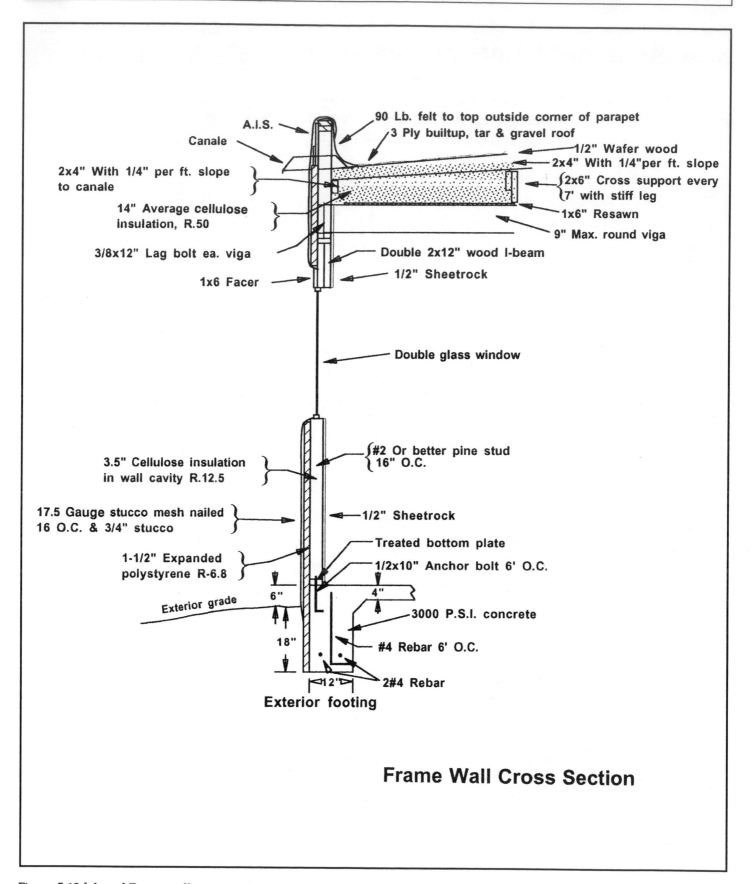

A.I.S.

Canale

90 Lb. felt to top outside corner of parapet

3 Ply builtup, tar & gravel roof

1/2" Wafer wood

2x4" With 1/4"per ft. slope

2x6" Cross support every 7' with stiff leg

1x6" Resawn

9" Max. round viga

2x4" With 1/4" per ft. slope to canale

14" Average cellulose insulation, R.50

3/8x12" Lag bolt ea. viga

1x6 Facer

Double 2x12" wood I-beam

1/2" Sheetrock

Double glass window

3.5" Cellulose insulation in wall cavity R.12.5

#2 Or better pine stud 16" O.C.

17.5 Gauge stucco mesh nailed 16 O.C. & 3/4" stucco

1/2" Sheetrock

1-1/2" Expanded polystyrene R-6.8

Treated bottom plate

1/2x10" Anchor bolt 6' O.C.

Exterior grade

6"

4"

3000 P.S.I. concrete

18"

#4 Rebar 6' O.C.

2'

2#4 Rebar

**Exterior footing**

**Frame Wall Cross Section**

Figure 5:13 [above] Frame wall cross section.

## FRAME HOUSE WALLS

We build exterior frame walls with structural lumber—studs, headers, framing members. Inside the frame walls run the electric lines, the plumbing, and often the heating ducts. In addition, the inside cavities are filled with cellulose insulation.

The structural part of the wall itself is built with standard 2" x 4"s (16" on center) or 2" x 6"s (24" on center). All these framing members can be cut from 9" trees. [See Figure 5:13.]

The headers (essentially lintels over openings in the walls), however, are commonly built of 2" x 12"s, requiring the cutting of larger, older trees. There is a high demand for structural lumber, including headers. The industry standard for headers is double 2" x 12"s of hemlock fir, which creates a market of millions of boardfeet. This is no longer necessary.

Manufactured I-beams in varying, large dimensions, including 2" x 12"s, are available. I-beams are sometimes cheaper to use, and they are uniform— without knots and cracks. Fewer I-beams can be used to hold some loads, and they are available in spans up to 24' (a 9" viga spans up to 18' without additional corbels). The larger spans are important in garages, which have a standard 20' span. [See Figue 5:14.]

Eventually, recycled framing members will be available more widely and less expensively than they are today. In the past, plywood has been made from larger trees, but it is now possible to make plywood from 9" trees (which can be grown on tree farms in seven years). But, to date, these products are still unreasonably priced or difficult to get.

Structural studs are being made of recycled plastic, and they are stronger than the best heartwood (one of the beliefs about heartwood is that the old growth forests, and therefore the old big trees, have the best heartwood—the strongest). With the advent of recycled plastics, however, the issue of strength goes away. The plastic products are strong. They are easier to work with, are exactly the right shape, are uniform in strength, and have no chipped corners or knots to deal with. However, plastics when made new, use finite petroleum resources, and they emit toxic gasses when they burn.

In frame houses, the outside wall of rigid insulation is installed over the structural studs. While wood studs have fair

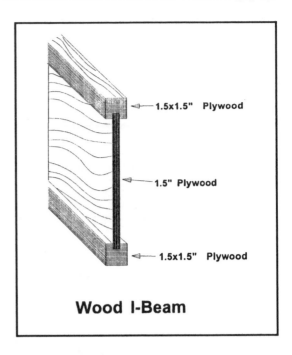

1.5x1.5"   Plywood

1.5"   Plywood

1.5x1.5"   Plywood

**Wood I-Beam**

Figure 5:14 [above]
Wood I-beam.

Figure 5:15 [above]
Exterior frame walls with
rounded/uneven edges.

insulating properties, the rigid insulation improves them significantly, providing R-7.5. This extra insulation also makes the
house quieter. Stucco netting is attached over this insulation by
driving standard 3" lathing nails into the studs, and stucco is
applied as the finish. The stucco itself is applied in three coats.
The corners of the walls can be cut to be rounded like a traditional adobe house. [See Figure 5:15.]

Because we insulate the outside of a frame T.R.E.E. home,

we do not need or use plywood at the corners of the house for bracing (increasing racking strength) as is most common and acceptable to code. We do use angle iron bracing on all exterior frame walls to compensate for plywood's strengthening qualities, and to allow for the use of bullnose (used for making rounded corners). This enhances the rigidity of the walls, which allows a building to withstand windshears that tend to push the walls out of square (racking strength), and minimizes hairline stucco cracks so common to frame/stucco buildings. We also use this technique on some long interior walls to increase the overall strength of the house. [See Figure 5:16.]

Figure 5:16 [below]
Wind bracing: Angle iron vs. plywood.

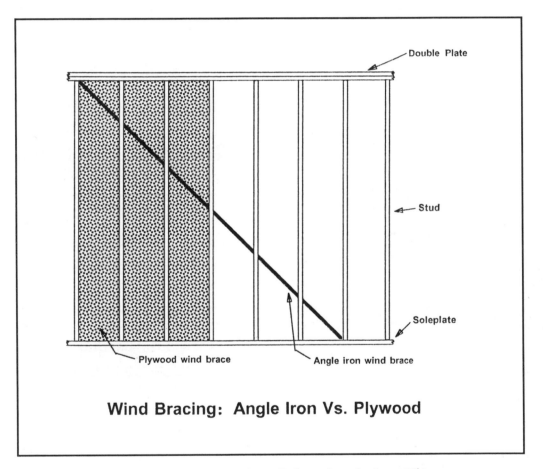

**Wind Bracing: Angle Iron Vs. Plywood**

The wall cavity is filled with cellulose insulation. This borate treated product is stable, inexpensive, fire retardant, and easy to install. The cellulose is mixed with glue, blown into the cavity, and when done, it is airtight and ensures no settling. It has the highest fire retardant rating and, as mentioned, boron is also nature's pesticide. Boron is hypo-allergenic, with no reported adverse side-effects for humans. The 3.5" of cellulose adds R-15 to the walls, making the walls ultimately R-22.

The interior side of a frame wall is made of gypsum board (sheetrock) and then painted, usually with latex paint. Gypsum is a relatively harmless product from an environmental standpoint. However, it *is* mined and is a finite resource.

Interior walls, except for adobe accent walls, are of frame construction. The electric lines and the plumbing in adobe houses are run through the interior frame walls, where possible. The load-bearing walls use I-beams as headers, just like the exterior walls. Cellulose insulation is added to some interior walls primarily for sound proofing—usually between bedrooms, bathrooms, and living areas. The walls are covered with gypsum board and painted. Even frame construction can be finished in aesthetically pleasing ways. [See Figures 5:17 and also Figure 2:5.]

Figure 5:17 [below]
Arched doorway in frame wall.

## FLOORS

Floors should be strong, yet resilient. They must resist transference of cold and moisture, be cleanable and highly wear-resistant, prevent vapor migration, and be resistant to insects.

Many homes are built with the base floor made of concrete. We minimize our use of concrete due to its high energy consumption and high levels of pollution. We use it only in our foundations, in stucco, and as the underfloor where carpet or tile will be laid. Concrete has several other characteristics that do not make it an ideal building material. Concrete allows vapor migration and often transmits water directly from the ground via capillary action. This is not a problem here in the arid Southwest but would be of greater concern in wetter climates. Also, concrete is not particularly resilient, which makes it less than ideal for flooring.

We recommend floors of brick laid on washed, graded, and compacted sand (standard mortar sand from local sand and gravel dealers), which ensures a flat floor surface. While the bricks are hard, and not resilient, their bedding in sand on earth allows for some "give." Termite and ant poison is applied to the sand, and a 6 milimetre, polyurethane membrane vapor barrier is installed before the bricks are laid, providing a safety barrier between the poison and the living spaces and an important vapor protection from the sand and earth beneath it. There is little chance of poison migration into the earth because water is needed to dissolve and carry the poison, and since no rain goes under the house or foundation it is a static condition. The house itself drains water away from this area. In areas where there is a high water table, however, other methods of protecting against poison migration would have to be used.

We recommend brick because it meets most of the qualities a floor must have, it is usually available locally, skilled masons are plentiful, and it provides a Southwest aesthetic many of us prefer. [See Figure 5:18.]

We also extensively use Saltillo tile floors, as they are similar in feel to brick but are inexpensive and environmentally kind. They also meet our Southwest aesthetic and design goals. [See Figure 5:19.]

Mud floors are indigenous to our part of the country. And many old homes still have mud or 'dirt' floors—caliche (dirt) hardens and wears very well after being sealed with urine or ox blood. Obviously, we no longer use urine or ox blood as sealers, but the idea of a sealed, colored mud floor is still viable. A combination of old ways and new technologies is particularly relevant regarding mud floors. The mud is here, and it's cheap. But, like the adobes, it needs to be stabilized to provide the durability we have come to expect in our home building materials. A mud floor, when finished, is hard yet resilient; it shines, and is easily cared for.

In addition to what we recommend for our T.R.E.E. homes in New Mexico, there are more than thirty materials used for floors—including wood, tile, linoleum, cork, asphalt, and rubber. Look to the indigenous peoples in your area for those materials most appropriate to your environment, and they will probably be of good quality at a low cost.

This is an area where recycling is taking hold—you can buy used bricks, recycled tile, or recycled carpet. Ask around.

Figure 5:18 [above]
Brick floor.

Figure 5:19 [below]
Saltillo tile floor.

ROOFS

*While we think of flat roofs as typically Southwestern, it has been estimated that 90% of all roofs, world-wide, are flat.*

We can think of the roof, as well as the ceiling, like we do the walls: inside, outside, and what's in the cavity. The ceiling/roof structure completes the box of the house that will allow us to regulate our environment, our weather. We can control air movement, temperature, humidity, precipitation, and sound.

The support for the roof must be strong enough to carry its dead load (the weight of the roof itself) plus whatever extra weight it might get on a regular basis—like snow, wind, and rain. The design and strength of the roof will prevent it from sagging. Just as we had concerns about the cold leaching into the house from the ground through the foundation (the reason we insulate the foundation so well), we have concerns about heat escaping through the roof. Much of the heat lost from a house in the winter (which of course is wasted heat, money, energy, and fossil fuels) is lost through the roof. So, we believe the roof needs superior insulation, at least R-50 and possibly high as R-70 or R-80 in colder climates such as Santa Fe or Taos.

Our T.R.E.E. home has functional as well as traditional aesthetic design elements. We incorporate traditional Southwest features into our ceilings, and our roofs usually are of the "flat" pueblo style, but behind the parapets, the actual roof is designed with a compound slope to provide 100% roof drainage. While we think of flat roofs as typically Southwestern, it has been estimated that 90% of all roofs, world-wide, are flat. So this design element should have wide application. [See Figure 5:20.]

The good news about Southwestern-designed ceilings is that they call for unprocessed timber, either in the form of vigas, roughcut planks and beams, or latillas. As mentioned before, vigas are the traditional roof/ceiling supports, made from hand-hewn logs left exposed in the room, and latillas are smaller "branches" used instead of planks as the decking for the ceiling. Some old-style vigas, however, were huge, often much larger than 12" in diameter. Today's concerns about the cutting of old growth forests makes the use of these large logs simply not acceptable to us anymore. We have developed a technique that allows us to deliver the function and design elements we want in a passive solar house, based on using logs no wider than 9" in diameter (a size that can be grown on tree

Figure 5:20 [top left]
Pueblo style roof line.

Figure 5:21 [bottom left]
Viga and roughcut ceiling.

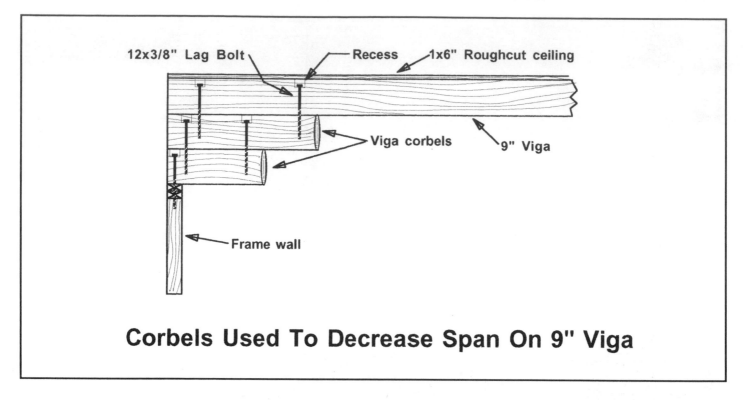

**Corbels Used To Decrease Span On 9" Viga**

Figure 5:22 [above]
Corbels used to decrease span
on 9" viga.

farms in seven years.) The use of roughcut timber reduces energy consumption because the lumber is less processed—it is not planed and it is air-dried rather than kiln-dried. In addition, roughcut lumber is produced locally, whereas most planed lumber comes from Oregon and Washington increasing, at minimum, the shipping costs and use of energy. [See Figure 5:21.]

Our use of wood ceilings improves the insulating properties of the ceiling/roof system, and increases the sound muffling qualities of the house, making for a quieter environment. The 9" diameter (at breast height) vigas we use span up to 18'. [See Figure 5:22.]

For spans larger than 18', we use corbels under the vigas to spread the weight, increasing the effective span. We have built 26' spans by stacking up to 3 corbels (of diminishing length) under each end of each viga. We use lag bolts, huge screws, to attach the corbels securely to each other and to the vigas. [See Figure 5:23.]

Since the pueblo style roof is flat, it is not an especially functional design if built absolutely flat. The pueblo style house has parapets (firewalls) around the outside walls at the roofline, and canales to drain the water from the roof. If, however, the roof is truly flat, it won't drain all the water. And over time the roof may sag and form ponds and puddles—not a healthy sit-

Figure 5:23 [above]
Vigas and corbels with latillas
as decking.

Figure 5:24 [left]
Compound slope roof.

uation at all. The roofs on our T.R.E.E. homes are of a compound slope design to provide 100% water runoff by building up parts of the roof and sloping it toward the canales (traditional drain spouts through the parapet wall for roof drainage). The canales themselves have decorative wood coverings made from pieces of 2" x 6"s. [See Figures 5:24 and 8:12.]

The roof consists of the ceiling (vigas and roughcut planks or latillas as decking), a cavity averaging 14" in depth, and the exposed exterior. The cavity is of varying height—based on the stiff leg stands placed every 4'—and forms the compound slope, as well as works with the 2" x 4" framing to support the exterior roofing system. Rafters that are 2" x 4" and 2" x 6" cross supports hold up the OSB (oriented strand board, or wafer

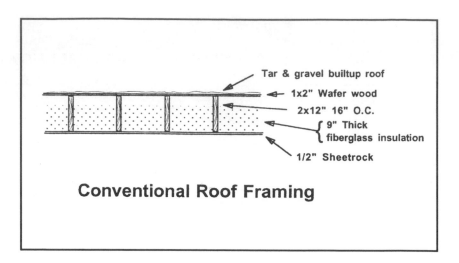

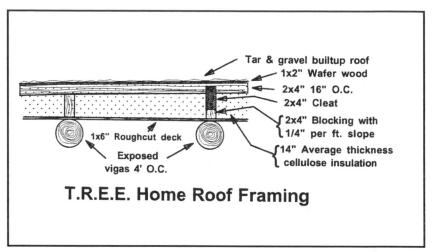

Figure 5:25 [top right]
Conventional roof framing.

Figure 5:26 [bottom right]
T.R.E.E. Home roof framing.

wood), a plywood type material, which is covered with fiberglass felt and 3-ply tar and gravel, ensuring a long-lasting water barrier. OSB can be made out of waste lumber from mills and the logging industry, as well as from trees grown on tree farms. [See Figures 5:25 and 5:26.]

This fiberglass roof is applied up the sides of the parapets, continuing on the top almost to the outside corner. Waterproof building paper is then wrapped over the parapet and down almost to the gravel roof, and then stuccoed. This double sealing eliminates "parapet leaks" so common in standard construction. When there are parapets within the roof that separate living areas, they are completely roofed up the sides and over the top, and then are stuccoed. Fiberglass, like glass itself, is a nasty material to manufacture, but our options are limited by our demand for high quality. Fiberglass is not, however, hazardous to install.

The cavity built between the ceiling and the roof is filled

FIGURE 5: 27     **ROOF/CEILING COMPARISON**

|                    | Standard Frame          | Double Roof                                     | Adobe Roof                  | Viga Roof                        | Compound Slope                                              |
|--------------------|-------------------------|-------------------------------------------------|-----------------------------|----------------------------------|------------------------------------------------------------|
| **Support Beams**  | 2" x 12" Surfaced       | Roughcut                                        | 6" x 10" Roughcut Corbels   | 9" Vigas, Corbels                | 9" Vigas, Corbels                                          |
| **Decking**        | Plywood/ Sheetrock      | Roughcut planks                                 | Roughcut planks             | Roughcut decking boards          | Roughcut decking boards                                    |
| **Insulation**     | Glass fiber batts       | Glass fiber batts                               | ISO rigid                   | Cellulose                        | Cellulose                                                  |
| **Roofing**        | Tar + Gravel            | 2" x 10" surfaced, plywood, tar + gravel        | AIS, tar + gravel           | AIS, tar + gravel                | 2" x 4", 2" x 6" OSB, fiberglass felt, AIS, tar + gravel   |
| **R-value**        | **R-30**                | **R-30**                                        | **R-30**                    | **R-30**                         | **R-50**                                                   |
| Kwh                | 17,725                  | 16,436                                          | 1788                        | 1131                             | 1260                                                       |
| Bdft               | 5,555                   | 11,953                                          | 7272                        | 6816                             | 6923                                                       |
| Acres              | 1.6                     | 3.4                                             | 2.1                         | 1.9                              | 1.9                                                        |

Figure 5:28 [top right]
Standard skylight.

Figure 5:29 [bottom right]
Curb mount skylight.

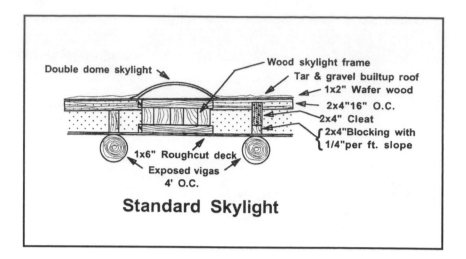

**Standard Skylight**

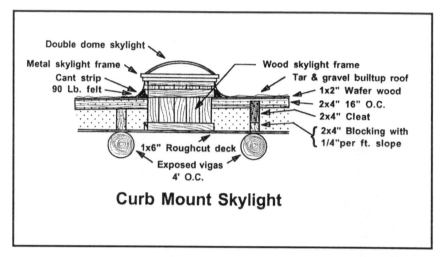

**Curb Mount Skylight**

with loose cellulose, a blanket averaging 14" thick. It is blown into the cavity and fills all the nooks and crannies batt insulation misses. Batt insulation is not "loose" but manufactured in standard sizes and shapes, and while it can be manipulated and compacted to some extent, it leaves gaps where there isn't a perfect fit. Near chimneys, furnace vents, and other "hot" exits from the house, the cellulose is held back by metal or wood "walls" so heat will not build up in the insulation around these hot vents. The finished ceiling/roof has an R-value of 55, but with some settling it becomes R-50. A house, while benefiting from lots of insulation and air-tightness, should not be completely air-tight. Some infiltration is necessary and desirable. This is done in T.R.E.E. homes via chimneys, bath ventilators, dryer vents, and the usual leakage around doors and windows. [See Figure 5:27 on page 71.]

Our skylights are the curb-mount type, which are built like the parapets. They are sealed with 90 lb felt, making them less

Figure 5:30 [top left]
Curb mount skylight: Exterior.

Figure 5:31 [bottom left]
Skylight: Interior using roughcut timber.

likely to leak. The curb-mount type of construction makes them easy to repair should they need it. [See Figures 5:28, 5:29, 5:30, and 5:31.]

Clerestories are used for heat gain and light, but they are expensive to build and, to some extent counteract their beneficial heating properties. To accommodate clerestories, a ceiling/roof must be raised, and heat dissipates at 1.5° per foot, ( 6'=8° drop in temperature at floor). ■

# 6 CHAPTER

# OTHER CONSIDERATIONS

All the aspects of building that did not fall directly into the building of the shell of the house are discussed here, at least specifically where we've developed techniques that are earth-sensitive.

## UTILITIES

As our T.R.E.E. homes are planned to be passive solar and use building techniques that minimize the use of energy, this section is really a summary. But, in addition to all those savings, we do recommend the use of gas forced-air furnaces and, where feasible, gas appliances such as water heaters. Gas is more energy-efficient (easily 70%+), is the best way to transmit energy, and is less polluting than oil and electricity. Additionally, there are still vast resources of natural gas, and there is very little loss in its transportation.

## WELLS AND SOFT WATER SYSTEMS

Many of the homes we build have their own wells, and many of the sites are in the Rio Grande River Valley of New Mexico, and are, thus, subject to relatively high water tables. Every site has its own specific issues about water for drinking as well as irrigation (water for landscaping).

If a well is needed, use the best well people available. In areas of high groundwater, where the well is deeper, knowledgeable drillers will mud pack the pipe to ensure that the top, polluted levels do not mix with the deeper, cleaner water you will drink.

For those who want soft water systems, we run soft water to all indoor faucets except the cold water lines to the kitchen and the ice maker. We do not run soft water to these lines to avoid potential health risks. The naturally hard water also runs to the outside hose bibs. We build a dry well, a separate drainage system for the soft water system, so the discharge does not interfere with the well or the septic systems. We recommend using a regeneration agent that is not salt, which over time can damage the earth and infiltrate into the groundwater. One agent that can be used with existing systems is K-Life, which uses potassium chloride rather than sodium chloride.

## BACK-UP AND SECONDARY SYSTEMS

Although our T.R.E.E. homes are primarily heated by solar energy, there will be times when the solar energy available is less than desirable (three or more straight days of overcast skies will limit solar benefits). Gas forced-air heating for the entire house is our choice, as the burning of gas is less damaging to the environment than oil and is much cheaper than electricity. Electricity is most often produced using oil or coal, which pollutes. It takes more gas to generate electricity than to provide heat directly. We recommend the use of mercury bulb-type thermostats rather than the lower quality, bi-metal ones, because they are more sensitive, reduce the potential for overheating, and thus, are more efficient.

Evaporative coolers are installed because they are extremely efficient and effective in cooling the air and provide some humidity in our dry climate. Manufacturers are now applying this efficient technology to refrigeration-type air conditioners as well.

## FIREPLACES

Fireplaces were once used for truly functional purposes, for heating and for cooking. They are not efficient for either pur-

pose today and they contribute to air pollution. There are lots of alternatives for fireplaces that are more economical: a well-insulated house; a wood burning or pellet burning stove; and gas fireplaces which are cheaper and contribute less to pollution. Yet many of us still want fireplaces. We continue to believe "they heat twice," physically and emotionally. So, fireplaces are an important emotional and aesthetic issue. [See Figure 6:1.]

Our fireplaces are built for high efficiency as well as beauty. They are usually hand-made, kiva (rounded into a corner) types with a steel door and screen. During construction, wood is not allowed close to the fire box by blocking out the framing. Non-combustible mineral board is installed behind fireplaces for an added measure of protection. All kiva fireplaces have combustion air intakes built into the exterior walls of the fireplace, venting to the outside. These vents may have their own dampers to reduce air flow when not in use. The steel door prevents heat loss up the chimney long after the fire is out. [See Figure 6:2.]

But we also use pots, Mexican pots, for fireplaces, sometimes even in bathrooms. [See Figure 6:3.]

Figure 6:1 [facing page]
Traditional kiva fireplace with hand-troweled plaster and banco.

Figure 6:2 [below left]
Kiva fireplace in kitchen.

Figure 6:3 [below right]
Decorative pot fireplace in bathroom.

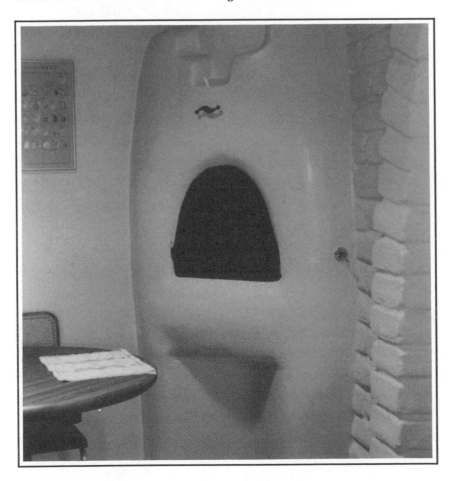

## GRAY WATER SYSTEMS

Gray water is the water draining from sinks, tubs, showers, and washing machines, not the septic effluent from toilets. In many areas, regulations stipulate that gray water must be run through the septic or sewer systems, but some communities are more flexible. Gray water systems are simple and fairly economic to install, and they are good for your gardens. Sometimes using gravel filled "sinks" or trenches, called French drains, diverts this "semi-clean" water directly into the earth. Water that contains grease (from the kitchen sink or the dishwasher) is run through the black water system that also handles drainage from the toilets. We believe that residences should have and use gray water systems where they are allowed, and that eventually homes will also have "constructed wetlands" to handle the black water sewage. [See Figure 9:1 and Chapter 9 for more details.]

## SEALERS

Overall, we do not like sealers from an environmental standpoint, but sometimes they are necessary or they are demanded by customers. We seal brick floors, exposed wood that does not weather well or is subject to insect infestations, and we seal adobes before painting. We use stucco, which uses cement, because replastering mud walls every year is unrealistic and makes for an unacceptable level of maintenance. We use latex rather than oil-based paints. Pursuing safer, highly effective sealers is one of our current top priorities.

## PLUMBING FIXTURES

We recommend cast iron/porcelain bathroom fixtures and the use of pressurized pipes of copper with lead-free solder. We also search out used fixtures—old tubs and sinks, even faucets—that can be cleaned up or reglazed. Often, these older fixtures add charm and a sense of history to a new home. [See Figure 6:4.]

## METALS

We use metal, but most of it is low grade and/or recycled. Virtually all the nails used are from recycled cars, trucks, or trains. Some steel is used, where its strength or heat resistance is demanded—as lag bolts to connect ceiling vigas and corbels, as rebar in foundation cement, as angle iron bracing in frame structures, and as fire doors for fireplaces. It has been estimated that as much as 90% of these common metals are from recycled material. ∎

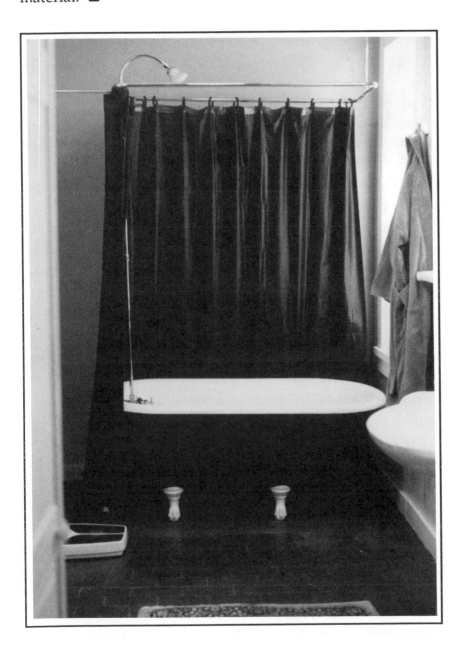

Figure 6:4 [left]
Recycled claw-foot tub.

# 7 CHAPTER

## THE TIRE HOUSE

We are in the process of building tire houses in the sand hills of Corrales, New Mexico. The exterior walls are made of steel-belted radial tires (that cannot be re-treaded) filled with compacted earth. Our tire house is the result of our years of building, and our years of experimenting and developing new, better techniques and ways to build environmentally responsible homes. This project is more than just a house built of tires. We have used more recycled materials than ever before and are installing a "constructed wetlands" for recycling sewage effluent from the house.

A tire house needs no foundation if the earth is adequately compacted, reducing significantly our use of concrete. However, as this is still an experimental building type and our local regulations are conservative, we must build a foundation. We can still reduce our use of concrete by using tires underground as part of the foundation. In the sand hills of Corrales, New Mexico where one tire house has been built, "undisturbed" earth is normally 80-85% compact sandy loam. The sandy loam under this house has been compacted to a density of 98% to a depth of 2'. A "modified bitumen" moisture barrier has been installed around the exterior walls to ensure that no water infiltrates under the walls even though water does not effect sandy loam's compaction or stability. Rigid waterproof insulation (12" x 1/5") has been installed around the exterior walls to ensure against freezing under the foundation, although freezing under the walls cannot undermine their structural integrity. [See Figure 7:1.]

The exterior walls have been made with steel-belted radial tires, which are free, at the moment. A company in Albuquerque, Acu-Tread Re-Tread, gives us the tires they cannot remake (by retreading or recapping) into tires with a "like new" failure rate. It saves them disposal costs and saves us as well. One of the problems associated with tires in landfills is that they decompose at a very, very slow rate. This is a benefit to builders because of the virtually non-existent side effects of decomposition (i.e. leaching and outgassing from rotting materials.)

The tires are kept stretched open until the earth is compacted within each tire. They are stacked simply, one atop another. The spaces between the tires have been filled with adobes cut to fit the space, or with extra bricks. The mixture of tires and adobes appears to be ideal—adobes are used to fill-in where the tires are too big or too small. Poultry netting (chicken wire) is used to hold all the pieces together. The wall is essentially tires, adobes, and rammed earth. The outside is then

Figure 7:1 [below]
Tire wall cross section.

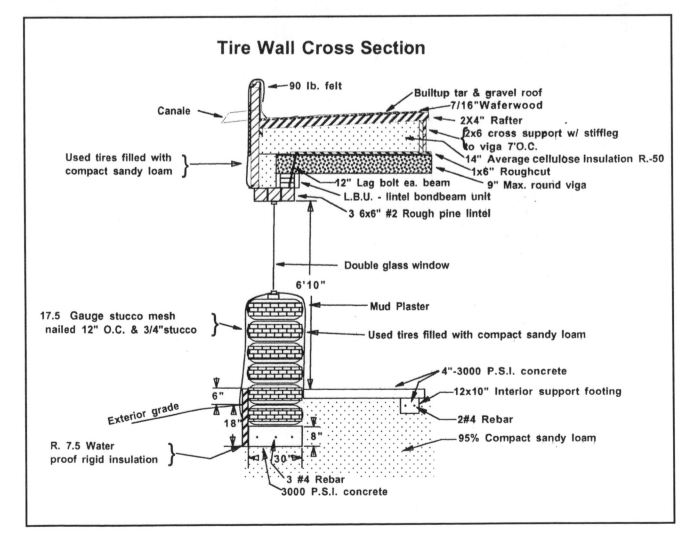

Figure 7:2 [above]
Tire house wall: Tires, adobes,
rammed earth.

wired and stuccoed. The extensive use of dirt in the tire wall and sealing of stucco makes it highly fire resistant. [See Figure 7.2.]

The mass and thickness of these walls makes these structures very stable. The exterior walls of the tire house are 30" thick. A typical frame house has 4" thick walls and a standard adobe wall is 10" (a double adobe is 20"). Every window sill is practically a window seat. The thermal mass of the exterior walls also eliminates the need for polystyrene insulation under the stucco, reducing the depletion of stratospheric ozone.

A particularly appealing aesthetic aspect of the tire house is the way we stack the tires, with the larger tires on the bottom. This, of course, provides greater stability to the walls, but also gives the outside walls a more dynamic line. In some old adobe houses the walls seem to "puddle" toward the bottom. The tire house will have some of this same effect. [See Figure 7.3.]

Aluminum thermal-break windows are used. These windows, as mentioned previously, require low maintenance and will last for a very long time. Structural wood components (vigas, decking, roof structure, parapets) will all be roughcut

Figure 7:3 [facing page]
Tires stacked to "puddle" at bottom.

Figure 7:6 [facing page]
Tire house floor plan.

Figure 7:5 [above]
Electrical lines in tire wall.

Figure 7:4 [below]
Great Room with vigas in place.

(low processing energy) and locally grown (low transportation energy). [See Figure 7.4.]

Some of the floors will be "mud" rather than brick, and interior walls will have traditional mud plaster, all low energy processes. Other floors will be Saltillo tile or carpeting made from recycled soda bottles, and the counter tops will be of Talavera tiles.

A "constructed wetlands" will be added to the standard septic system to eliminate ground water pollution from the septic tank. [See Chapter 9 for more details and Figure 9:1.]

The plumbing lines were laid in first and, where required, will run up the interior frame walls. The electrical lines, however, lie naturally in the spaces between the tires. [See Figure 7:5.]

When completed, the tire house will look like other T.R.E.E Homes. And the layout is similar to our other homes as well. [See Figure 7:6.] ∎

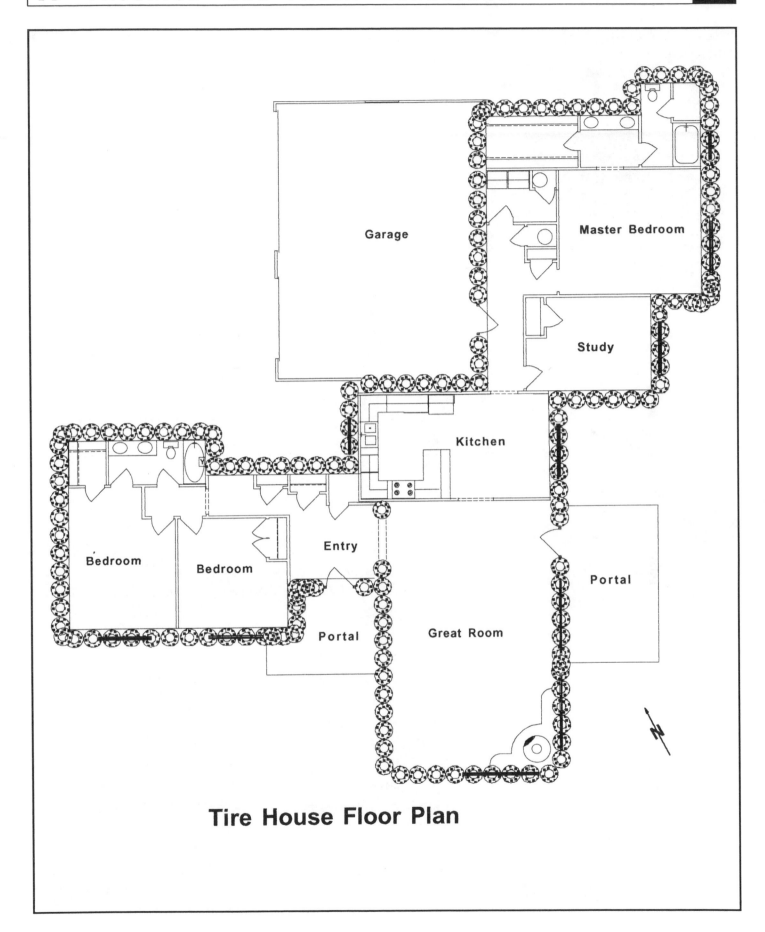

**Tire House Floor Plan**

# 8  CHAPTER

# EXAMPLES OF T.R.E.E. HOMES

Here are details about the decisions made in designing and building two different T.R.E.E. homes: one adobe and one frame.

The layouts of the two houses were, originally, virtually identical. They both were oriented for solar gain with the living room and bedrooms facing south. Each house was approximately 1850 square feet. [See Figure 8:1.]

And the costs for each house were essentially the same, once inflation and land costs were taken into account. The cost of the original home was approximately $165M. The adobe T.R.E.E. home was built in the sand hills of Corrales, New Mexico. Its orientation was to provide views of the Sandia mountains to the East while securing strong solar benefits. [See Figures 8:2 and 4:1.]

Because this house was built in the sand hills, the foundation chosen was the standard T.R.E.E. home foundation for adobe houses. The inside dimensions of this house are smaller than the frame house discussed below because the exterior adobe walls are thicker (10" vs 4"). One half square foot of living space is sacrificed for every linear foot of adobe wall.

The adobe house was built in 1989 and brick floors were used throughout. Two fireplaces were built, with one in the kitchen/dining area. The ceilings were vigas and roughcut planks. Only one window was built facing West, from the kitchen, and it was protected by a covered portal at the entry. [See Figure 8:3.]

Only one small window was built in a North wall, in the

Figure 8:1 [facing page, top]
Typical T.R.E.E. Home floor plan.

Figure 8:2 [facing page, bottom]
East side elevation.

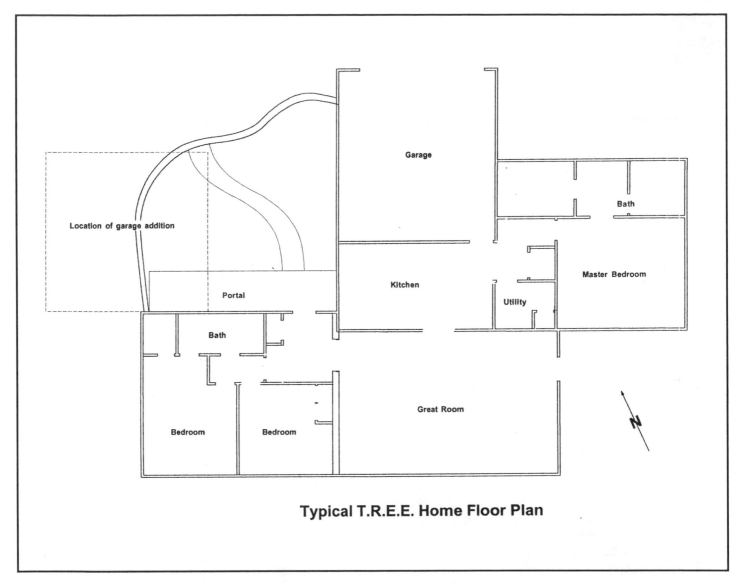

**Typical T.R.E.E. Home Floor Plan**

**East Side Elevation**

master bath to provide light. Eventually, a portal was added to the East side of the house.

The frame T.R.E.E. home was built in the lowlands of Corrales amid the remaining trees of a one-hundred-fifty-year-old apple orchard. Saving these trees was a primary consideration and the 3/4 acre lot was long and narrow. So the house was angled on the land, providing adequate solar orientation and "fitting"the house into the stand of trees. Additionally, this angling of the house [See Figure 4:3.] provides a greater sense of space going into the house and looking out at the contained view of the old apple trees. [See Figure 8.4.]

This house was built with greater interest in its resale value. And because it was so close to the street, greater attention was paid to "street interest."  The roof line near the entry

Figure 8:3 [above]
Northwest portal at entry.


Figure 8:4 [facing page]
Contained view of old apple orchard.

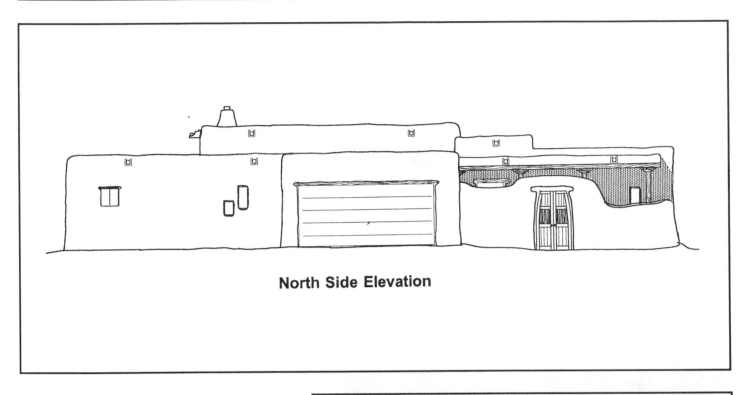

**North Side Elevation**

Figure 8:5 [facing page]
Three level pueblo style roof line.

Figure 8:6 [above]
North side elevation.

Figure 8:7 [right]
Small north side windows for light
and "street interest."

Figure 8:8 [top right]
Talavera tiles used in the kitchen.

Figure 8:9 [bottom right]
Talavera tiles used for the shower.

was designed with three levels—the entry and the living room ceilings were raised at increased expense to provide this aesthetic element. [See Figures 8:5 and 8:6.]

Figure 8:10 [above]
Vigas and latillas ceiling.

Small windows were added to the North wall, facing the street, for street interest and to provide light into the closets. These small windows take the place of skylights, which were used on the adobe house discussed previously. [See Figure 8.7.]

This house was built of frame construction in 1991 because it was cheaper and faster, and we had a sub-contractor who knew our framing techniques. The foundation of this house took extra effort. Because the land in the flats has more clay, the earth under each footing was dug out more than three feet and filled with sand. The clay, when wet, becomes too plastic, whereas sand will hold its compact form better.

Saltillo tiles were used on the floors throughout, rather than bricks, as we were trying to use cheaper and more environmentally safe products. Talavera tiles were used on the counter tops, back-splashes and for the shower/sunken tub. These tile elements are good for resale as they are perceived as Southwest Style. [See Figures 8:8 and 8:9.]

Figure 8:12 [above]
Canale covered with wood.

Figure 8:13 [below]
Outside sconce light made from Mexican pot.

The ceilings were made with vigas, roughcut planks or latillas, again with resale in mind. [See Figure 8:10.]

The corbels used on the portal were made of 2" x 6"s rather than the traditional 6" x 6"s. This reduces the use of large-dimensioned lumber. The design we developed for these corbels has a recessed center piece which enhances the aesthetics of the corbel. [See Figure 8:11.]

These same pieces of 2" x 6" are used for canale covers as well. The canale itself is metal. [See Figure 8:12.]

The outside sconce lights were made from Mexican pots cut in half, again a design decision that seems typically Southwest, is inexpensive, and does little damage to the environment. [See Figure 8:13.]

After purchase, the owners converted the original garage to make an artist's studio with north light and added a garage to the west.

Both T.R.E.E. homes have very low utility bills in a climate that gets snow and freezing in the winter and temperatures above 100° in the summer. ∎

| FIGURE 8:14 | **AVERAGE UTILITY BILL COMPARISON** | | | |
|---|---|---|---|---|
| | 1850 Sqft Adobe | | 1850 Sqft Frame | |
| | Gas | Elec. | Gas | Elec. |
| Average Monthly Bill | $26.47 | $53.46 | $27.65 | $43.25 |
| | 25 months | | 15 months | |

Figure 8:11 [left]
Corbel "relief."

# 9 CHAPTER

# THE FUTURE
# Alternative
# Design

The techniques and processes described below are in use now but they are not widely practiced. These techniques are a mixture of returning to very old ways, turning current problems into resources, and taking advantage of natural resources.

We, as builders and consumers, can push industry to change its basic ways—to look for alternative materials and to recycle and reuse virtually everything it can. At the same time, we must continue to use renewable natural resources for more and more products. Solar power and wind power are the easiest for us to deal with currently.

## BUILDING MATERIALS

The new movement in building materials is the use of garbage—old tires (for our tire house), and plastic. Both tires and plastics are major issues in garbage disposal because they decompose at very, very slow rates. Thus, they create current and long-term problems in terms of natural recycling. Newspapers also decompose at surprisingly slow rates, but we are using recycled newspapers in cellulose insulation and consumers are recycling newspapers more and more.

Plastics last a long time and use a lot of energy resources to produce. It makes sense, therefore, to use them where their durability and long-lasting qualities are important. Recycled plastics are being used to make park benches, carpet, and structural building studs. Carpets are now available made from old ketchup bottles. The plastic is extruded into fine fibers and woven into carpets. Instead of using lumber for 2" x 4"s or 2" x 6"s inside the walls of the house, plastics can be used. At the current time plastic studs are not reasonably priced, but, as with many new technologies, we expect the costs to come down as manufacturers make their processes more efficient and demand picks up. So, look for recycled plastics; they may be more available than you think.

The use of 9" trees or smaller is very important. This recommendation has been spread throughout the book, but we all must continue to ask about products made from smaller trees grown on tree farms or sustainable managed forests. Structural framing materials can be made from smaller trees, so can decking planks, wafer wood, and vigas. So can plywood. Many of the products available are reasonably priced, so search them out.

Earth houses—in this case *bermed* (partly buried into the earth) or *sod houses*—have been around for a long time. Both types grew out of primitive building practices—from living in caves and cliff dwellings, to pit houses and raised houses with natural roofs (grasses and tree branches). Like the old cliff dwellings, [See Figure 1.1.] bermed houses usually face south and are built right into the north hill. The earth keeps the shelter cool. However, these houses are not cost effective.

Bermed houses seem "easy" to build, but they are not. It is a massive job to hold back the earth so the house can be stable. Insulation is needed to protect the house from the cooling properties of the earth. Earth maintains a temperature of approximately 66°. Water retention against the house from the earth is also an issue, so French Drains must be installed. The result—a massive, drained, insulated retaining wall is built. An expensive proposition.

Sod houses are often bermed, but essentially they use dirt and grasses as the roof tops. These are often prairie houses, where sod is easily available. The use of sod on the roof is, again, a good way to insulate a house and protect the house from the weather.

Essentially what these, and other, houses have in common is the use of materials that are "right there." Wherever you are there are materials that are readily, easily, and inexpensively available. These construction techniques arose out of using what was near at hand. In ancient times transportation was difficult if not impossible, so people used native resources. We can do

*We, as builders and consumers, can push industry to change its basic ways— to look for alternative materials and to recycle and reuse virtually everything it can.*

the same.

In South Dakota there is a house made of corn cobs. Corn cobs are also being used as part of an aggregate cement mix, as are rice hulls and sawdust. By-products, recycling, inexpensive materials—builders are now investigating ways to use naturally occurring waste from their own local environments.

In Nebraska, Arizona, and New Mexico there are houses made of straw bales. Straw is waste product for many farmers who grow grain for seed. It is estimated that two hundred million tons of straw are burned every year, contributing smoke to the high levels of pollution already present. Straw has much more thermal mass than frame construction, and somewhat less than adobe or tire/earth walls. Straw bales will make walls between 18" and 24" thick. They are fire resistant because the bales hold enough air for good insulating properties, but not enough for easy burning. We believe the straw bales should be mixed or sprayed with boron for even greater fire resistance and to prevent the decomposition of the straw from mold, mildew, and vermin. We are interested in this technique as one of our future experimental projects.

We are also interested in using building blocks made of recycled paper—paper adobes. The process is now being perfected in southern New Mexico. We are also involved in developing a rigid form of cellulose insulation.

Tires, beer cans, and bottles: houses have been built using all these materials. Mike Reynolds of Taos, New Mexico, has spent twenty years developing techniques that use steel-belted tires rammed with earth as the exterior wall material. He has also built homes using beer cans laid in cement. His homes are designed to be self-sufficient. He calls them "Earthships" and has built more than eighty of them.

Builders using many of these materials extol their abilities to insulate houses better than traditional materials; their durability (many of these "new-fangled" homes have been standing for hundreds of years), and their low cost.

## RECYCLING EFFLUENT AT HOME

As with the gray water systems discussed in Chapter 5, recycling waste water (gray or black) may involve local government agencies, permits, and regulations. And, yet, slowly, things are changing. More and more people are installing gray water and personal sewage treatment systems.

Constructed wetlands are, like the tire house, currently hot subjects. These systems are essentially ponds and marshes built to allow nature to recycle waste, the most efficient and beneficial process. Currently, we dump sewage into the ground via septic systems, and into our water via sewage treatment plants. We do not effectively or efficiently process this waste. And with the earth's population expanding all the time, we need to find old/new ways to do things better. In Arizona, the Biosphere II project theoretically is completely self-contained. The people living in Biosphere II grow all they need and recycle all their waste. In Arcata, California the sewage treatment system involves the use of a one-hundred-fifty-four-acre wetlands park, which dumps the treated effluent, ultimately clear water, into Humbolt Bay. This water ends up cleaner and clearer than the water already in the bay.

Residential wetlands are essentially gravel lined beds, with an impermeable membrane at the bottom to contain the sewage in the treatment area. Native wetland plants like reeds and cattails are planted in the beds. The bacteria living near the roots of these plants thrive on the swampy water dumped into the pond they live in. After this "natural treatment," the water is clean and can be used for irrigation or discharged into the ground. An added benefit is that wetlands attract waterfowl,

Figure 9:1 [below]
Constructed wetlands.

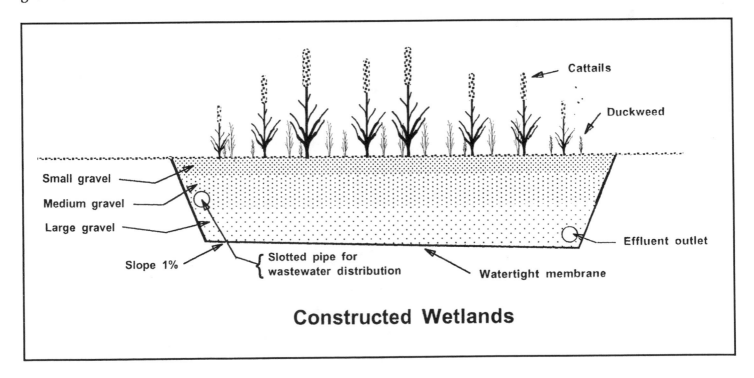

**Constructed Wetlands**

creating residential wildlife refuges, another benefit to earth's dwindling wild habitats. [See Figure 9:1.]

## ENERGY RESOURCES

Essentially, we go back to solar power and wind. We believe in harnessing the natural powers available to us. We build passive solar houses, but we are moving in the direction of active participation. We have found that using more insulation (R-22 in the walls and R-50 in the ceiling) and accessing more direct solar gain through south facing windows, are the best and cheapest ways to conserve energy. They are easiest to use in building and, ultimately, the most cost effective, even with backup systems in place. Trombe walls are no longer cost effective compared to a well-insulated house with direct solar gain.

In the 1970s we thought active solar power was the answer, but twenty years later we are still looking for ways to make it easier to collect and use, less costly, and more aesthetically acceptable (smaller, integrated into the building in less obtrusive ways).

Work is being done to develop roofing materials that will contain the collectors for solar energy. They will essentially be invisible and the systems will be simpler and better. The batteries are being made more efficient and houses can be wired for this energy source. DC wiring can be added at little cost for lighting (not yet for outlets), but this signals movement forward. Another oil shortage or embargo will increase the attractiveness of this idea. The Japanese, who are more dependent on foreign oil than we are, are actively pursuing this photovoltaic technology.

Wind has been used for hundreds of years to run the pumps of water wells. You see wind mills all over the west still. In California there are wind farms, with high tech wind mills made in Japan. A natural force that can be used. Again, though, this will probably not be a major energy source in the next few years, but it is clean, available, and can be harnessed.

Heating our homes is done in a variety of ways, as we've suggested. Construct a well-built, well-insulated house; orient it appropriately to the sun; use natural gas furnaces as a back-up system. But many people still use wood to heat their homes, in fireplaces and wood stoves. From an environmental standpoint, wood burning is not all bad. Wood is a renewable resource and burning wood, as long as replacement trees are grown, is not a net contributor to global warming (growing trees absorb more $CO_2$ than is released by burning wood). Fireplaces can be built more efficiently than they usually are, and wood stoves are being improved all the time. One of the current hot items in stove heating is the pellet stove, which uses pellets made of compressed sawdust or other agricultural waste products. The burning of the pellets contributes significantly less pollutants to the environment than the burning of wood. In many communities where wood burning is regulated (no burn days when wind factors make the pollution worse), pellet stove burning is exempt. The problem currently with pellet stoves is the expense, both in terms of purchasing the stove itself and the price of the pellets. These costs will probably come down in the future.

We continue to encourage manufacturers to pursue more environmentally responsible methods of making plywood, glue, stains, dyes, polyiso insulation, and cement. We also are interested in alternatives to metals.

This is only a sampling of what the future may hold. There are always people out there trying new things, trying the old ways again, looking for a better, cheaper way. When they become "tried and true" rather than experimental, we incorporate them into our building practices. You can do the same. ■

# Appendix

FIGURE A: 1   **R-VALUES/ U-VALUES OF SELECTED MATERIALS**

| Material | | R/U-Value |
|---|---|---|
| **Building Boards, Panels, Flooring** | | |
| Gypsum or plaster board | 3/8" | .32 |
| Gypsum or plaster board | 1/2" | .45 |
| Plywood | | 1.25/ inch |
| Sheathing, wood fiber | | |
| (impregnated or coated) | 25/32" | 2.06 |
| Wood fiber board | | |
| (laminated or homogenous) | | 2.38/ inch |
| Wood fiber, hardboard type | 1/4" | .18 |
| | | |
| **Building Paper** | | |
| Vapor-permeable felt | | .06 |
| Vapor-seal, 2 layers of mopped 15lb felt | | .12 |
| | | |
| **Finish Materials** | | |
| Carpet and fibrous pad | | 2.08 |
| Carpet and rubber pad | | 1.23 |
| Terrazzo | 1" | .08 |
| Gypsumboard (sheetrock) | 1/2" | .45 |
| Gypsumboard (sheetrock) | 5/8" | .56 |
| Hardwood flooring | 25/32" | .68 |
| | | |
| **Insulating Materials** | | |
| Blankets and Batts: | | |
| ..Mineral wool, fibrous form | | |
| (from rock, slag, or glass) | | 3.12/ inch |
| ..Wood fiber | | 4.00/ inch |
| Boards and Slabs: | | |
| ..Cellular glass | 90° | 2.44/ inch |
| Glass fiber | 30° | 4.55/ inch |
| Expanded polyurethane | | |
| (R-11 blown; 1"thick or more) | 25° | 5.88/ inch |
| Expanded polystyrene, extruded | 30° | 4.17/ inch |
| Expanded polystyrene, molded beads | 30° | 3.85/ inch |
| Loose fills: | | |
| ..Macerated paper or pulp (cellulose) | | 3.57/ inch |
| ..Mineral wool | 30° | 4.00/ inch |
| ..Perlite (expanded) | 30° | 2.94/ inch |
| ..Vermiculite (expanded) | 30° | 2.27/ inch |
| ..Sawdust/ shavings | | 2.22/ inch |

* U-Values.
U-Values are the reciprocal of R-Values.

## FIGURE A: 1    R-VALUES/ U-VALUES OF SELECTED MATERIALS (cont'd)

| Material | | R/U-Value |
|---|---|---|
| **Masonry Materials-Concretes** | | |
| Cement mortar | | .20/ inch |
| Lightweight aggregates | | |
| (pumice; perlite or vermiculite) | 60lb/ft | .59/ inch |
| Stucco | | .20/ inch |
| **Masonry Units** | | |
| Brick, common | | .20/ inch |
| Concrete block, 3 oval core (cinder aggregate) | 8" | 1.72 |
| Concrete block, rectangular core | | |
| (Sand and gravel aggregate, 2 core, 36lb) | 8" | 1.04 |
| **Roofing Materials** | | |
| Asbestos-cement shingles | | .21/ inch |
| Asphalt roll roofing | | .15/ inch |
| Built-up roofing | 3/8" | .44 |
| **Siding Materials** | | |
| Stucco | | .20/ inch |
| **Woods** | | |
| Hardwoods (maple, oak) | | .91/ inch |
| Softwoods (fir, pine) | | 1.25/ inch |
| **Wood doors - Solid core** | 1-1/4" | 1.82 |
| **Still air** | | |
| Horizontal, air flow up. Reflective surface | | 1.32 |
| Non-reflective surface | | .61 |
| Horizontal, air flow down. Reflective surface | | 4.55 |
| Non-reflective surface | | .92 |
| 45° slope, air flow up. Reflective surface | | 1.37 |
| Non-reflective surface | | .62 |
| 45° slope, air flow down. Reflective surface | | 2.22 |
| Non-reflective surface | | .76 |
| Vertical, air flow across. Reflective surface | | 1.70 |
| Non-reflective surface | | .68 |

* U-Values.
U-Values are the reciprocal of R-Values.

FIGURE A: 1   **R-VALUES/ U-VALUES OF SELECTED MATERIALS  (cont'd)**

| Material | R/U-Value |
|---|---|
| **Moving air** | |
| 15 mph wind, any direction. Winter. | |
| Non-reflective surface | .17 |
| 7.5 mph wind, any direction. Summer. | |
| Non-reflective surface | .25 |
| **Windows and Skylights *** | |
| Single pane flat glass. Winter | 1.13* |
| Summer | 1.06* |
| Insulating glass. Double | |
| 3/16" air space. Winter | .69* |
| 3/16" air space. Summer | .64* |
| 1/4" air space. Winter | .65* |
| 1/4" air space. Summer | .61* |
| 1/2" air space. Winter | .58* |
| 1/2" air space. Summer | .56* |
| Storm windows. 1-4" air space. Winter | .56* |
| Summer | .54* |
| **Horizontal panels** | |
| Plastic bubbles. Single walled. Winter | 1.15* |
| Summer | .80* |
| Plastic bubbles. Double walled. Winter | .70* |
| Summer | .46 * |

* U-Values.
U-Values are the reciprocal of R-Values.

FIGURE A:2   **R-VALUE/ U-VALUE COMPARISON**

| | Standard | | T.R.E.E. HOME | | |
|---|---|---|---|---|---|
| | Frame | Adobe | Frame | Adobe | Tire |
| Foundation | 4 | 4 | 6.8 | 6.8 | 6.8 |
| Wall | 13 | 13 | 25 | 25 | 14 |
| Ceiling | 30 | 30 | 50 | 50 | 50 |
| Windows * | 1.5 | 1.5 | 1.5 | 1.5 | 1.5 |
| Doors | .75 | .75 | .75 | .75 | .75 |

* U-Values.

# Glossary

# A

Above grade:       see Grade

Adobe:             Sun-dried bricks of sandy earth,
                   mixed with clay, water, and sometimes
                   cement or asphalt emulsion to stabilize
                   them against deterioration by weather.

Active Solar:      Solar energy collected, stored, and used
                   employing mechanical systems.

AIS:               Asphalt impregnated sheathing.

# B

Below-grade:       see Grade

Bermed house:      Structure built partly into the earth.

Biosphere:         A complete, self-sustaining biological system.

Black water:       Waste water containing human waste,
                   as sewage.

Bondbeam:          Beam of wood or cement laid along the top
                   of a masonry wall to support the ceiling beams
                   and spread their weight evenly along the
                   length of the wall.

Bullnose:          Rounded corner/edge (hand troweled with
                   cement or plaster or stucco, or rounded
                   metal used with sheetrock/ dry wall.)

# C

Canales:           Drain spout, usually rectangular, through
                   the parapet wall for roof drainage.

Cement:            The binding agent that holds sand and
                   other aggregates together in a hard,
                   stone-like mass.

CFC:               Chlorofluorocarbons

Checking:          Cracks in timber

Cladding:          Covered (clothed)

| | |
|---|---|
| Compressive strength: | Pressed together, compacted strength. Resistance to compressing/ crushing. |
| Concrete: | Artificial stone made by mixing cement, sand, gravel or other aggregate, and enough water to cause cement to set and bind the entire mass. |
| Console: | Structural block used to raise height of roof/ceiling support. |
| Constructed wetlands: | An artificial, man-made, marsh used to absorb and treat (purify) water. |
| Corbel: | A short structural member placed under a main support beam to decrease the span of the main beam. |
| Cupping: | Wood that has warped into a cup-shape. |

# D

| | |
|---|---|
| Dead weight (load): | The weight of the structure and its built-in furniture/appliances. |
| Deciduous: | Plants that lose their foliage seasonally. |
| Decking: | The material forming a deck (i.e. the ceiling itself). |
| Direct gain: | Heat derived directly from the sun's rays. |

# E

| | |
|---|---|
| Ecosystem: | Interactive biological system. |
| Effluent: | Outflow of liquid, such as water or sewage. |
| Evaporative cooler: | An air-conditioning system based on evaporation, especially useful in arid climates. |

# F

| | |
|---|---|
| Footings: | The foundation—steel reinforced concrete base of a wall, usually wider than the wall, to spread the weight of the wall/ structure over a wider area and to span possible voids in the earth. |

French drains:      Perforated pipes used underground to
                    collect and direct water away from the
                    structure.

# G

Global warming:     Allowing the greenhouse effect to go out of
                    balance, increasing the temperature of the
                    atmosphere/earth.

Grade:              The upper surface of the earth beside the
                    finished structure.

Gray water:         Waste water that does not include sewage
                    (i.e. showers, sinks).

Gypsum Board:       Sheetrock/ dry wall.

# H

HCFC:               Hydrochlorofluorocarbons.

# I

I-beam:             Structural member made of metal, plastic,
                    wood—whose cross section resembles the
                    letter "I."

# L

Latex paint:        Water based, rather than oil based, paint.

Latilla:            Small "branches" or trees, peeled or unpeeled
                    used as decking for ceilings and other
                    decorative uses.

LBU:                Lintel bondbeam unit. A structural member
                    used as a combination lintel and bondbeam.

Lintel:             A horizontal member spanning an opening
                    to carry a superstructure.

Live weight         Flexible, not fixed, weight—people, furniture,
(load):             wind, rain, and snow.

Load bearing strength:  The ability of a structure to hold weight.

# O

O.C.:  "On center" measurement point.

OSB:  Oriented strand board. Similar to plywood, made with chips or small pieces of wood glued together with grain running in same direction.

Outgassing:  Slow, continuous leaching of vapors after production.

Ozone:  Gas that comprises the upper layer of atmosphere (stratosphere).

# P

Passive Solar:  Solar energy used without mechanical collection and storage.

Photovoltaics:  The mechanical systems (silicone wafers) that generate electricity directly from solar radiation.

Planed lumber:  Wood that is surfaced.

Plywood:  Wood made up of an odd number of veneer sheets glued together with the grains, usually, at right angles to each other.

Portal:  Porch.

PSI:  Compressive strength expressed in pounds per square inch.

# R

Racking strength:  Ability to hold shape, to hold square.

Rebar:  Metal bars made with high tensile strength steel, used for reinforcing, especially concrete.

Roughcut:          Dimensioned lumber (beams, posts, or boards)
                   usually without any bark, cut out of logs at
                   the sawmill.

R-Value:           A figure to measure a material's resistance
                   to heat flow—the higher the R-value the
                   better the insulation properties.

# S

Solar:             Pertaining to the sun.

Surfaced lumber:   Roughcut lumber which has been
                   additionally processed, dried and planed
                   to get lumber with stable dimensions mainly
                   for framing (beams, studs, plates).

# T

Trombe wall:       A masonry wall with unvented glazing (glass)
                   placed in front of it to create a greenhouse
                   effect that increases the temperature of the
                   wall itself. The heat radiates into the house at
                   night when the outside temperature falls.

# U

U-value:           The reciprocal of R-Value

# V

Viga:              Peeled, unsawn log, used as support beam.

VOCs:              Volatile organic compounds.

# X

Xeriscape:         Landscaping designed to survive without
                   water or fertilizer, usually native plantings
                   of the climate.

# Bibliography

## BOOKS:

Bank of America. *Getting Down to Earth (an environmental handbook)*. N.p.: Bank of America NT&SA, Bank Investment Securities Division, 1972.

Chang, Amos Ih Tiao. *The Tao of Architecture*. Formerly Titled *The Existence of Intangible Content in Architectonic Form Based upon the Practicality of Laotzu's Philosophy*. Princeton, NJ: Princeton University Press, 1981.

Duncan, S. Blackwell. *The Dream House Think Book*. Blue Ridge Summit, PA: Tab Books, 1977.

The EarthWorks Group. *50 Simple Things You Can Do To Save The Earth*. Berkeley, CA: Earthworks Press, 1989.

The EarthWorks Group. *The Next Step: 50 More Things You Can Do To Save The Earth*. Kansas City, MO.: Andrews and McMeel, A Universal Press Syndicate, 1991.

Gray, Virginia; Macrae, Alan; McCall, Wayne. *Mud Space & Spirit: handmade adobes*. Santa Barbara, CA: Capra Press, 1976

Kern, Ken. *The Owner-Built Home*. Completely Updated and Revised. New York: Charles Scribner's Sons, 1975.

Klein, Hillary Dole & Wenner, Adrian M. *Tiny Game Hunting: Environmentally Healthy Ways to Trap and Kill the Pests in Your House and Garden*. New York: Bantam Books, 1991.

Loken, Steve; Spurling, Walter; Price, Carol. *GREBE: Guide to Resource Efficient Building Elements*. Missoula, MT: Center for Resourceful Building Technology, 1991.

Mazria, Edward. *The Passive Solar Energy Book: A complete guide to passive solar home, greenhouse and building design*. Emmaus, PA: Rodale Press, 1979.

McHenry Jr., Paul Graham. *Adobe: Build It Yourself*. Revised Edition. Tucson, AZ: The University of Arizona Press, 1985.

*New Mexico Home Energy Guide*. N.p.: New Mexico Energy, Minerals and Natural Resources Department and the New Mexico Research and Development Institute Communications Office at the University of New Mexico, 1989 and 1993.

O'Connor, John F. *The Adobe Book*. Santa Fe, NM: Ancient City Press, 1973.

Pearson, David. *The Natural House Book: Creating a healthy, harmonious, and ecologically-sound home environment.* New York: Simon and Schuster, 1989.

Rossbach, Sarah. *Feng Shui: The Chinese Art of Placement.* New York: E.P. Dutton, 1983.

Southwick, Marcia. *Build With Adobe.* Revised and Enlarged Second Edition. Chicago: The Swallow Press, 1974.

Tatum, Rita. *The Alternative House: A Complete Guide to Building and Buying.* N.p.: Book Developers, Inc., 1978.

Taylor, PHD., Anne. *Southwestern Ornamentation & Design: The Architecture of John Gaw Meem.* Santa Fe, NM: Sunstone Press, 1992.

Warren, Nancy Hunter. *New Mexico Style: A Source Book of Traditional Architectural Details.* Santa Fe, NM: Museum of New Mexico Press, 1987.

Wells, Malcolm. *Gentle Architecture.* New York: McGraw-Hill Book Company, 1982.

Wright, Frank Lloyd. *The Natural House.* N.p.: Horizon Press, Inc., 1982.

## ARTICLES, JOURNALS, REPORTS:

Best, Don. "Building with borate." *Popular Science Magazine.* N.p., March 1988 (?).

"Building by the Bale." *People Magazine.* New York: Time-Warner, Inc., 1992.

Dahir, Mubarak S. "Mfrs. Response Mixed to Possible R-123 Toxicity." *Energy User News.* Radnor, PA: The Chilton Company, August, 1991.

Dahir, Mubarak S. "CFC Disposal Problem Turns into $260K Profit for Sara Lee." *Energy User News.* Radnor, PA: The Chilton Company, August, 1991.

Eauclaire, Sally. "Straw Houses No Fairytale." *New Mexico Magazine.* N.p.: April 1993.

Grist, Charles; Karmous, Moustafa. "Energy Use and Conservation in Oregon's Lumber and Wood Products Industry." Salem, OR: Oregon Department of Energy, March 1988.

Kress, Stephen. "It's a Rocky Road to Rio: Senator Al Gore Offers An Earth Summit Assessment." *Crosswinds: New Mexico's Newsmonthly*. Santa Fe, NM: Crosswinds, June 1992.

Lemonick, Michael D. "Showdown in the Treetops: Conservation activists stage a high-altitude sit-in to save the ancient forests." *Time Magazine*. New York: The Time, Inc. Magazine Company, 28 August, 1989.

Linthicum, Leslie. "The Earthships Have Landed." *Albuquerque Journal*. Albuquerque, NM: Albuquerque Publishing Co., 2 August 1992.

*Los Angeles Times*. "Timber Industry Study Says Spotted Owl Thriving." Albuquerque Journal. Albuquerque, NM: Albuquerque Publishing Co., 19 August 1989.

Lloyd, Brian A. "Environmental Assessment: Mining and Reclamtion Plan for the White MesaGypsum Mine, Centex American Gypsum Company, Sandoval County, New Mexico." Albuquerque, NM: Department of the Interior, Bureau of Land Management, Albuquerque District Office, Rio Puerco Resource Area, January 1986.

Papineau, David. "In the Footsteps of the Dodo." Review of *The Diversity of Life*, by Edward O. Wilson. *The New York Times Book Review*. New York: The New York Times, 4 October 1992.

Robertson, David K. "Expanded Revision of Effective U-Values: U-Values for Opaque Wall Sections, Glazing, and Passive Solar Wall Types." Final Report. Albuquerque, NM: New Mexico Research and Development Institute, November 1981.

Schinkel, Jorg. "Aiming for the T.R.E.E. House (Timber Reduced, Energy Efficient House)." Corrales, NM: Passage Construction Company, November 1989.

Stewart, Doug. "Nothing Goes To Waste in Arcata's Teeming Marshes; A California town proves that ingenuity is a match for high-tech engineering in turning sewage into a natural resource." *Smithsonian Magazine*. N.p.: April 1990.

USDA Forest Service. "Environmental Impact Statement, Santa Fe National Forest Plan." N.p.: USDA Forest Service, 1987.

USDA Forest Service. "Summary of the Environmental Impact Statement for the Santa Fe National Forest Plan." (Final Environmental Impact Statement). N.p.: USDA Forest Service. 1987.

USDA Forest Service, Southwestern Region. "Santa Fe National
     Forest Plan." N.p.: USDA Forest Service, 1987.

Vogel, Peter. "The Greenhouse Effect." *Reddy News, The Energy
     Communication Magazine.* Albuquerque, NM: Reddy Commu-
     nications, Inc., July/August 1988.


## ENTIRE NEWSLETTERS, MAGAZINES, OR SPECIAL EDITIONS:

*Environmental Building News: A Bimonthly Newsletter on Environmen-
     tally Sustainable Design and Construction.* Brattleboro, VT: West
     River Communications, Inc., July/August, September/
     October, November/December, 1992.

*The Good Life: Crosswinds Guide to Healthy, Environmentally-Conscious
     Living.* Santa Fe, NM: Crosswinds, June 1992

Index

# About the Authors

## ED PASCHICH

is an owner of Passage Construction Company, Inc., builders of custom homes in Corrales, New Mexico. Passage Construction consists of Ed, his father, Jack, and other family members. Jack grew up in an adobe home in Columbus, New Mexico and had a dream of building modern adobe homes. Ed learned basic construction in Austin, Texas. In 1976 Ed and Jack formed Passage Construction and have been building passive solar adobe homes in the high desert of the Southwest ever since. They analyzed materials and developed construction techniques over the years as they built homes—custom homes, adobe homes, frame homes. They experimented, improved their skills and methods, and developed specific ways to be more in tune with the environment. The concept presented in this book is a direct result of their desire to be environmentally responsible.

## PAULA HENDRICKS

is a well-known writer and photographer living in Corrales, New Mexico. Her own line of museum quality notecards featuring her photographic images is retailed nationally. She has just completed a major renovation of her frame/stucco home—a project that took a year. In this process she had to deal with many of the issues presented in this book.